Childhood Learning, Behavior, and the Family

CHILDHOOD LEARNING, BEHAVIOR, AND THE FAMILY

By
LOUISE C. TAICHERT, M.D.

HUMAN SCIENCES PRESS
Formerly *BEHAVIORAL PUBLICATIONS INC.*
72 FIFTH AVENUE, NEW YORK, N.Y. 10011 • (212) 243-6000

Library of Congress Catalog Card Number 72-11521
Standard Book Number 87705-039-2
Copyright © 1973 by Behavioral Publications
Reprinted 1976 by Human Sciences Press

HUMAN SCIENCES PRESS
72 Fifth Avenue,
New York, N.Y. 10011

Printed in the United States of America
654321   98765432

Library of Congress Cataloging in Publication Data

Taichert, Louise C
    Childhood learning, behavior, and the family.

    Bibliography: p.
    1. Learning, Psychology of. 2. Learning ability.
3. Problem children. 4. Problem family. I. Title.
[DNLM: 1. Child behavior disorders. 2. Learning
disorders--In infancy and childhood. 3. Parent-child
relations. LC4661 T129c 1973]
LB1051.T157   370.15'2   72-11521
ISBN 0-87705-039-2

Table of Contents

Foreword

This book originated from a new subspecialty of pediatrics which is limited to childhood learning and behavior problems. My interest began with a primary concern with behavior and the ways in which it is influenced by learning ability and problems associated with it.

The ideas presented have emerged through a series of self-enlightening experiences that have been similarly shared by my colleagues. One soon becomes aware of the serious disruptive effects of children's learning problems on the normative development of family life and the sometimes catastrophic consequences on the emotional health of the child. To help children and their families to avoid these problems, one must go beyond the evaluation of the child and learn about his family and how to work with both. Changes must occur in the family system in order to effect change in a child; therefore, the child and his family must be regarded as a functional unit.

The therapy described in this book proceeds from a process-oriented, non-categorical assessment of child development and family function. This provides information about what is going on with the child and family so that something can be done. Thus, labels are avoided, since one cannot treat a label or a symptom.

The purpose of this book is to share the ideas that have gradually evolved into a new neurodevelopmental-family discipline. The text can be used as a handbook for anyone who works with children--pediatricians, psychiatrists, psychologists, nurses, teachers, social workers, and family therapists. The ideas of the family system and the interactional patterns of communication, particularly as they relate to the child with learning problems, are elaborated and the approach is presented for its clinical application.

Case material has been used throughout the text to illustrate the use of this new discipline, as well as to demonstrate the dynamic function of the family system. Specific details of family histories, including names and ages, have been changed to preserve the privacy and confidentiality of the doctor/patient relationship.

This discipline has evolved in the Child Study Unit, Department of Pediatrics, University of California-San Francisco*, under the direction of Dr. Helen Gofman, a pioneer in childhood learning disorders, assisted by Dr. Alan Leveton, who had a prophetic interest in Gestalt-oriented family therapy and who possesses a genius for teaching. My original categorical interest in childhood learning has been expanded through my professional association not only with them but with Dr. Leon Whitsell (pediatric neurologist), Dr. Richard Flower (speech and language pathologist, Mrs. Wilma Buckman (psychiatric social worker and family therapist), Dr. Bayard Allmond (pediatrician and Assistant Director, Child Study Unit), Mrs. Alice Jane Whitsell (Director, Reading and Language Development Clinic, and Mrs. Donya Harvin (psychologist).

I would like to thank Mrs. Phyllis Brislawn, psychologist, who has worked closely with me in my private practice.

I would like to give special thanks to Anne M. Schmid, Editor, Department of Pediatrics, for her encouragement and excellent editorial assistance, and to Miss Jeanne Chouinard, my secretary, for her constant help.

Louise Taichert, M.D.

*The fellowship training program of the Child Study Unit is supported in part by the Maternal and Child Health Services Training and Study Project No. 144, Department of Health, Education, and Welfare.

Introduction

The two disciplines of child development and family therapy have been combined to form the basis for a neurodevelopmental-family approach to the comprehensive understanding and management of childhood learning and behavior problems. This system considers the need to understand the relationship between two important determinants of behavior and experience, i.e., the child's ability to learn and develop language function and his dynamic interaction within his own unique family system. In this approach, the child and family are considered together as a functional unit, with the child viewed as a growing organism with an ever-changing substrate in response to his own family system, and an assessment of these factors as part of the therapeutic process. An inherent part of this concept requires a focus on the child's neurodevelopmental state, for the child brings to life a biological constitution which sets the stage for many of the subsequent events of his life.

Although the child's innate ability to learn and develop language function and the dynamic interaction of the family system are two important determinants of childhood behavior and experience, these two concepts are rarely considered together in the clinical management of these problems. Rather, these ideas and others are often considered separately through the specialization of professional interests. The child is often seen apart from the family in individual psychotherapy, in the absence of a neurodevelopmental assessment and an evaluation of the family system.

The basis for an effective approach to the management of childhood learning and behavior problems is the comprehensive, process-oriented, non-categorical assessment of child development and family function. Through such an assessment an understanding is gained about where the child is in his learning and language development and how this relates to, and is affected by, communication, values, rules, roles, and myths within the family system. The assessment is the first phase of therapy, which begins with the first patient-consultant encounter, not as a separate process which starts at the close of an evaluation.

The child is considered to be in a state of neuro-developmental growth in dynamic response to environmental stimuli, demands and expectations. His tasks follow a developmental continuum and appear specific for each child as to rate and extent of growth. These growth tasks are associated with the development of higher associative cognitive and communication skills, as well as social adaptation. The communication skills include the development of expressive language and speech, receptive language, acquired written language skills (reading, writing, spelling, arithmetic), neuromotor skills, sensory integration, awareness and discrimination. The tasks of social adaptation involve the development of autonomy, emotional security, and growth of inter- and intrapersonal and interfamily relationships.

An understanding of the behavior and development of a child is also dependent upon his nutritional state (prenatal and postnatal); his natural genetic endowment (innate biological constitution) which includes the ability to learn, and his innate activity level as an expression of the neurophysiological state; response to the kinds of sensory stimuli presented; emotional nurturence; environmental control (parental); and the dynamic functioning of the family itself. Recognition of these many complex factors does not imply focus on a single variable or viewpoint, even though a single viewpoint is usually established by specialty interests of medicine and psychiatry and is reflected by teachers, counselors, nurses, social workers, psychologists and family therapists in their work with children. Pediatricians and neurologists, for the most part, have been trained to focus on the organic or neurological effects of behavior with categorical interest in mental retardation and specific learning disorders, whereas psychiatrists have been primarily concerned with the emotional aspects of the critical mother-child relationship. From the tendency to specialize, an adversary dilemma has developed into therapeutic cults or camps of either/or-ism. This polarization of interest in either emotional or neurological etiology has continued the nature-nurture conflict even into the "multidiscipline diagnostic team approach" where an attempt has been made to bring several disciplines together. With this conflict between ideas of causality and treatment, e.g., emotional vs neurological, mind vs body, content vs process, Freud vs Perls, etc., the patient is caught somewhere in the middle. Views such as these have been responsible for many of the myths held in clinical practice, which offer false hope for parents in search of help.

There are two commonly held mental health models, medical-disease and growth. The traditional method most widely used in child psychiatry, pediatrics and neurology falls within the framework of the familiar disease mental health model. This reflects the need for structuring, labeling and categorizing, processes which are inherent in this model. When this preoccupation with nosology (Korner & Opsvig, 1966) is not the investigative goal in itself, treatment is directed toward removal of a pathological condition or its symptoms. Once the illness is removed, a change is expected and it is assumed that the mis-spent energy will be used effectively in some other way. In the mother-child relationship, which is often considered pathological, the child is described as having some pathological state or complex which requires removal or treatment. There is a sense of finality in the use of diagnostic labels.

In the other approaches, usually, after someone other than the therapist collects the social history, the therapist begins to rescue the child from his mother by individual psychotherapy. Although individual psychotherapy for the child provides an often-needed ally in the therapist, it tends to blame the mother and isolate the child. This prevents the therapist and family members from observing themselves in interaction, and little attention is given to the relationship of the total family as a system and as a personality.

The terminology used in such classification of child-hood behavior problems was usually adapted from concepts and diagnostic categories of the adult disease psychiatric model. This child was frequently viewed as a small adult with small adult problems and pathology. For example, childhood autism was considered a form of schizophrenia (Berberich, Lovaas, Peiloff, & Schaffer, 1966; Kanner, 1943), whereas, in the new approach presented, the autistic child is considered to have psychoneurodevelopmental dysfunction which accounts for the disorder of affect and communication. The child has difficulty in relating to others and fails to use early language development as a meaningful way to communicate. He often demonstrates self-directed activity, rhythmic and twirling motions, preoccupation with objects, echolalia, and/or one of several misleading, isolated cognitive or language skills. These misleading strengths have led, heretofore, to a commonly accepted view that the child is emotionally disturbed as a result of poor mothering, which prevented or concealed normal learning ability, social adaptation, and communication skills. In fact, the child's neurodevelopmental state determines the quality of the mothering response (Rimland, 1964). The autistic child provides little, if any, satisfactory feedback to sustain maternal interest and stimulation. By treating this as a childhood form of schizophrenia with adult criteria, the child is considered to be emotionally disturbed. This immediately implicates parental blame, and calls for a course of traditional psychotherapy for the child rather than our present approach which calls for training and educational therapy for the child and supportive therapy for the family.

In recent years there has been a shift away from the disease model towards a growth model, i.e., change through growth (Ackerman, 1951, 1966; Bell, 1964; Bell & Vogel, 1968b; Perls, Hefferline, & Goodman, 1951; Perls, 1969; Satir, 1964). The increased understanding and acceptance of the growth model and its accompanying terminology bears a positive semantic impact of hope. The assessment of child development and family process inherently lends itself to the idea of growth, and provides information about what is going on in the family and where the child stands in his learning and language development. It, therefore, considers the behavioral consequences of this development. From an understanding of what and where comes an understanding of what needs to be done. This model eliminates the need for diagnostic labels, mysticism and assumption, and begins to meet the child's needs rather than those of the therapist. The idea that "the child could if he would" is replaced by the idea that "the child would if he could." The non-verbal child who has, in the past, been labeled "passive-aggressive with castration anxiety and assumed hostile motives for not wanting to speak" might now be considered a child with difficulty in speaking and an inability to put ideas and thoughts into words, or as one who lacks the words, vocabulary and the necessary sound formations. With difficulty in spontaneous verbal expression of ideas and feelings, he expresses anger and/or sadness as a consequence, problems which can be further complicated if the child lives in a family where open communication is not possible.

Learning and behavior are dependent on many variables and no single factor or relationship should be considered independently for a comprehensive understanding of childhood learning and behavior.

1 Critical Issues of Childhood Learning and Behavior
(Historical Review)

As an introduction to the understanding of childhood learning and behavior, a brief historical review of the critical issues of child development and family process is presented.

There are few persons in the field of child development who would doubt that all life's processes depend on heredity and experiential circumstances (Lipsitt, 1967). Yet, the nature-nurture conflict is carried into clinical practice and is still discussed (McBride, 1969) even though this argument was long ago considered empty and lacking in substance (Anastasi, 1958). In 1937, Katz ignored these issues altogether in his engaging and enlightened description of child development (Katz, 1937). He felt that the child shares with the animal a great subordination to the senses, but while the animal remains constantly under their control, the child frees himself step by step. At first the child lives in the present like the animal; however, he gradually breaks this fetter and learns to anticipate the future inwardly and to grope back into the past. The child frees himself from the restraints of the present by means of the play of free ideas. All our present knowledge leads us to suppose that the animal remains bound to the present.

Because man can learn so much and culture can shape his personality to such an extent, many believe that the phenomenon described by Katz is possible because the human brain is actually a "tabula rasa" (clean slate) (Eibl-Eibesfeldt, 1967) made for learning and that environment alone shapes behavior.

It is not difficult to demonstrate in principle that

1

this viewpoint is incorrect. In his article, "Learning and the Human Infant," Lipsitt (1967) describes a congenital response repertoire on which he feels all behavior change depends. He feels that the teachings of Freud ignored this congenital response by placing too great an emphasis on early experience in determining later behavior. Some contemporary methods of child psychiatry appear to embrace the viewpoint of a clean slate, when treatment is begun without an assessment of the child's inherent ability to learn. This idea considers all children to have the same potential and that they can blossom with the aid of proper experience and psychotherapy. The view of a clean slate cannot be upheld.

There are fixed action patterns and a congenital repertoire at birth, which are important determinants of learning and behavior and this behavior varies considerably from individual to individual (Wolff, 1967). Every newborn has its own sleep-wake cycle, hunger tolerance, activity level, state of arousal, etc.

Carmichael (1954) and Gesell (1954) favor a constitutional interpretation of development, and consider time and physiological maturation as primary determinants of behavior. Kessen (1967) and Eibl-Eibesfeldt (1967), in their studies of infant newborn behavior patterns, feel that the newborn is equipped with fixed action patterns, such as sucking, crying, and smiling, which appear to be innate behavior patterns (Freedman, 1965). Sucking is an innate response released by certain stimuli, i.e., hunger in the presence of a spontaneous seeking mechanism (Prechtl and Schleidt, 1950); in addition, rudimentary swimming, climbing movements, as well as the basic pattern of walking are fixed motor patterns (Peiper, 1953). The smiling response occurs initially quite spontaneously after the baby has been fed to satiation (Koehler, 1954), later in response to someone bending over him (even to crude dummies), and finally only to known persons (Spitz, 1946). Children born blind also show the smiling response and other basic expressive movements (Freedman, 1965; Goodenough, 1932; Freedman, 1964), and those born deaf start to babble like normal children but stop when there is no auditory feedback. Jespersen (1925) described the case of two neglected Danish children who grew up with a deaf grandmother and spoke with each other in a language of their own that bore no resemblance to Danish. They had invented it probably on the basis of an inherited learning disposition and given motor coordination.

There are many important issues to be considered in early human development--learning, psychosexual, social, etc. (See Table I on Comparative Phases of Development.) Some phases or issues are believed to be critical in determining subsequent learning and behavior, for example, gender role is thought to be assigned before the age of five years, despite the child's genetically determined sexuality (Freud, 1945; Stoller, 1969). If speech and language development is prevented through deafness or profound lack of appropriate stimulation within the first seven years of life, it is believed that little, if any, further development can occur.

Piaget (1936) studied and described the origins of intelligence as sequential phases of learning. One phase, for example, is the phenomenon of object-permanence which occurs during the first phase of learning around seven months of age when, for the first time, the infant immediately remembers and looks after an object lost from sight. The phase of autonomy between two and four years of age, when the youngster gains bowel and bladder control and other abilities of self-reliance, is one example of early social growth and adaptation described by Erikson (1950). Escalona (1962) studied individual differences and Sander (1962) described the longitudinal development of early mother-child interactional issues. Sander feels that each issue must be successfully completed for the success of subsequent issues. The infant, for example, establishes a firm object relationship with the mother at or around 18 months of age as one issue, and must subsequently learn to comfortably separate himself from his mother as another.

In the clinical management of childhood learning and behavior, the family as well as the infant's biological constitution and maternal-child issues must be considered. However, attention has been focused usually upon one single variable--the important relationship between one personality and another, in particular the mother and child.

Table 1

Comparative Phases of Development

Years	Erikson	Piaget	Freud (Psychosexual)	Years	Receptive Language Development	Expressive Language Development	Reading and Pencil Skills	Arithmetic Skills
						Language Skills		
0-1	Phase I: A Sense of Basic Trust	Sensori-motor Phase	Oral	0-1		First word, noun		
			Anal	1-2	Begins to relate symbol and object meaning; recognizes 120-275 words; inhibits on command	20-100 words; nouns, some verbs; single-word sentences		
2				2-3	Recognizes 400 at 2-1/2, 800 at 3; responds to commands, e.g., "jump up"	200-300 words; two-word sentences		
3	Phase II: Sense of Autonomy	Precon-ceptual Phase	Genital	3-4	Understands up to 1500 words by 4; recognizes plurals, sex differences, pronouns, adjectives; answers simple questions	900 words; verbs, nouns, pronouns, adjectives; three-word sentences	Copies circle	
4				4-5	Understands from 1500 to 2000 words; understands	Tells an organized story	Copies + in imitation	Counts to 4 by rote

Age	Psychosocial Phase	Cognitive Phase	Stage	Age Range	Vocabulary	Grammar	Reading	Arithmetic
6			Latency	6-7	2500 to 2800 words & complicated sentences	Approaching adult form	Identifies letters; copies triangle; prints name & identifies words	+; knows right from left
7				7-8		Good automatic grammar usage	Copies diamond; reads Durrell card #1	Adds and subtracts one-digit numbers
8				8-9			Reads Durrell card #2	Borrowing and carrying
9	Phase IV: Sense of Industry	Phase of Concrete Operations		9-10			Knows months of year in order; reads Durrell card #3	Simple multiplication
10				10-12			Reads Durrell card #5	Multiplication & simple division
12				12-15			Reads Durrell card #7	Long division; adds and subtracts fractions
13	Phase V: Sense of Identity	Phase of Formal Operations; Puberty & Adolescence						
19								
20	Phase VI: Sense of Intimacy							

Relatively little attention has been given to the relationship of the total family as a system and as a personality. The notion that the family is largely responsible for the ultimate development of childhood behavior and emotional health is a compelling one in contemporary behavioral science. In clinical practice, there is some awareness of family dynamics, but the family has been treated largely as a collection of separate individuals who affect the child's personality and development.

Vogel and Bell (Bell and Vogel, 1968b) look upon the family as a functional unit with functional problems analogous to those faced by society as a whole. They see the functions of the nuclear family as task performance, family leadership, integration, solidarity, and pattern maintenance. Each member of the family has a role in determining these functions. Each family has its own value system.

In Vogel and Bell's study of families with an emotionally disturbed child (1968a), each child had been used as a scapegoat and had specific problems on which the family could focus. Most of these children had primary problems in learning and were selected as scapegoats because they were a threat to the parents' achievement values. These observations concur with my own personal experience with the educationally handicapped child, who must handle his problems with learning as well as the problems that often result from his role as the family scapegoat. The educationally handicapped child as the scapegoat performs a valuable function for the family by channeling family tensions and providing a basis for family solidarity.

Since the personality of the child is acquired in part through the process of accepting those roles assigned to him by his parents, the child is particularly susceptible to deviant development and disturbed behavior when parents express their conflicts by assigning inappropriate roles in implicit ways (Kaufman, Peck, and Taguiri, 1954a and b). Assignment of roles is seen as a leadership function of the parents. The "emotionally disturbed" child's role as a problem child is generally supported by the parents' explicit criticism and implicit support of the persistence of what has been criticized. This is done by failing to follow through on threats, by delayed punishment, or through the continued use of double-level messages which place the child in a double bind (Satir, 1964).

The child with his own unique pattern of development then attempts to adapt to the growth landmarks established by the society in which the family exists. Until recently, each child has been expected, for the most part, to meet the same learning tasks at the same time. There is, however, a growing awareness that many of the children's problems can be avoided when each child is considered to be unique and that his own action patterns and learning behavior must be specially considered.

Nonetheless, the children with the greatest differences present the highest risk of becoming emotionally disturbed as casualties of mothering, education, or a dysfunctional family system.

With these issues in mind, a comprehensive understanding of childhood learning and behavior requires a view towards the many aspects of heredity and environment. The view, therefore, towards only the mother or child in the mother-child relationship is not enough. This relationship functions within a biological system which in turn functions within many other systems, e.g., family, school, political, economic, etc.

2 Specific Learning Problems

Although general interest in specific learning disorders has developed only recently, this problem was documented as early as 1896 when a British physician, W.P. Morgan, reported a case of congenital word blindness (Morgan, 1896). About 41 years later, Samuel T. Orton (1937), in his classic monograph on the relationship of reading disorders to other developmental language disorders, acknowledged the skill of reading as a developmental process and, later, Bender (1957) and Schilder (1960) introduced the idea that disabilities in reading could be explained partially on the basis of maturational lags. This latter view implies a temporary condition that can be outgrown, and accounted for the misleading optimism in the past.

Learning problems are generally considered to be emotional or neurological in origin. Depression, the stress of anxiety, fear, worry, preoccupation, inappropriate roles, family dysfunction, interfere with learning; and it is known that profound emotional and sensory deprivation in the infant and young child can disrupt normal neurodevelopment or result in irreversible neurodevelopmental dysfunction. The real problems, or inability to learn, are on an acquired or primary neurodevelopmental basis. So often, the emotionally disturbed child in clinical practice is the child with learning problems who experiences and expresses stress from a neurodevelopmental state which interferes with successful adaptation at home and at school.

The neurodevelopmental or neuroconstitutional learning problems fall into three categories: mental retardation, slow learning, and specific learning disabilities. The learning problems in any of these categories can be on a familial, metabolic, traumatic, infectious, cultural-economic, or unknown basis. Mentally retarded children

9

make up 3% of the total population and are identified with an arbitrary intelligence quotient (I.Q.) of 70 or less by standard testing (Scheerenberger, 1964). An even larger number of children are considered to be slow learners and fall within a grey zone of intelligence, with an I.Q. score falling between 70 and 90. Although children in any range of intelligence may show specific disorders of learning, those with an intelligence in the normal range but with significant difficulty in specific processes of learning are designated as having specific learning disorders. According to some estimates (LaVeck, 1970), 10% to 20% of the school population fall into this category and it is to this group that I confine my discussion.

The terminology that has developed from the diverse and vast literature on specific learning disorders has been confusing; the terms most widely used have been "minimal brain damage" (Eisenberg, 1957), "minimal cerebral dysfunction" (Gomez, 1967), and "minimal brain dysfunction" (Clements and Peters, 1962; Clements, 1966). I have a preference for a newer term, "neurodevelopmental dysfunction," since the idea of damage has disturbing implications. The etiology of these problems is often unknown and the specific focus of central nervous system involvement is not readily identifiable. These problems may be acquired as a result of neonatal or postnatal morbidity or may be inherited. In both the acquired and developmental forms of learning problems there appears to be a high incidence of prenatal, birth, and postnatal morbidity. The disorder of reading of genetic origin has been classified as "primary developmental dyslexia." The term dyslexia relates specifically to a disorder of reading. It is used by some to mean any disorder of written or spoken language, or as a cover-up for some other problem. According to one ophthalmologist, the problem has gained such popularity that "Parents live on the right side of town, drive a Mercedes-Benz, have braces on their children's teeth, and have one child with dyslexia (Institute for Development of Educational Activities, Inc., 1969).

A child with a specific learning disorder has normal intelligence on the Wechsler Intelligence Scale for Children (WISC) and demonstrates, by further evaluation, to have one or more determined disabilities in specific processes of learning which interfere with the development of acquired written or spoken language skills, e.g., reading, writing, spelling, arithmetic, and spontaneous expressive and receptive language (Taichert, 1968; Whitsell, 1969). These acquired language skills appear to develop in a continuum and, whenever this becomes disrupted, specific skills are delayed or develop unevenly.

The processes of learning which are most crucial in the early development of acquired written and spoken language are the visual and auditory processes of perception, discrimination, short- and long-term memory, meaningful and meaningless rote sequential memory, and motor integrative function. (See Table 2.) Disabilities in these processes are manifest in delays in specific areas of school achievement, often of two or more grade levels, and require special academic consideration. The use of tests that measure the function of these specific processes of learning help to define the child's learning style in terms of strengths and weaknesses; therefore, a formal assessment of these learning processes is necessary to determine the extent and nature of the disability. The information gained from this assessment will provide descriptive information about the child's ability to learn, mental age and school achievement levels which, in turn, alert the school and parents to the child's specific needs and will determine the specific course of remediation. An understanding of these issues demonstrates the important relationship between the child's ability to learn and develop language function and the manner in which he behaves and experiences life in his given family system.

The following review of the specific learning processes involved in the development of acquired written and spoken language skills (i.e., reading, writing, spelling, and arithmetic) will provide a better understanding of specific learning disorders and childhood learning. These necessary skills develop in a continuum, with a critical relationship between the skill being taught and the developmental appearance of specific learning processes. This relationship has a significant effect upon academic achievement and behavior and must be understood whenever childhood behavior and learning are being considered.

TABLE 2

LEARNING PROCESSES INVOLVED IN ACQUIRING READING SKILLS

DECODING	COMPREHENSION

VISUAL PERCEPTION
TACTILE-KINESTHETIC PERCEPTION
    Figure-ground discrimination
    Position of figure in space
    (d b p q g)
	AUDITORY PERCEPTION
	    Attention to auditory detail
	    Sound discrimination
	    Understanding meaning of
	    sounds and words

VISUAL MEMORY
TACTILE-KINESTHETIC MEMORY
    Memory for shapes and forms
    of single letters and whole
    words (visual gestalt)
	AUDITORY MEMORY
	    Short- and long-term
	    memory

VISUAL SEQUENTIAL MEMORY
    Meaningful--ability to remember
    several letters in right-left
    sequence to spell a word
 	
    Rote--ability to remember letters
    of the alphabet in order
	AUDITORY SEQUENTIAL MEMORY
	    Meaningful--ability to repeat
	    in order a series of heard
	    sounds that make up a
	    word or sentence
	    Rote--ability to say letters
	    or months of year in order
	    or count

VISUAL-MOTOR INTEGRATIVE FUNCTION
    Integrative process involving
    perception, memory, and
    fine motor coordination of
    the hands necessary for
    writing, drawing, and
    copying
	AUDITORY-MOTOR INTEGRATIVE FUNCTION
	    Writing from dictation, requiring
	    sound-symbol relationship

VISUAL-VOCAL INTEGRATIVE FUNCTION
    Naming letters and sounding out
    words
	AUDITORY-VOCAL INTEGRATIVE FUNCTION
	    Articulatory coordination for
	    speech and language
	    development

READING

In developing the Illinois Test of Psycholinguistic Abilities, Bateman and coworkers (1967) developed the theory that reading is learned in two stages: (a) symbol recognition and conversion of the written symbol to a sound which is dependent on the visual pathway and is primarily a process of decoding, and (b) comprehension and reading for meaning which is primarily dependent on auditory skills. They concluded that reading is essentially an auditory skill and that, although Stage I is primarily a visual decoding task, it should be taught by phonic and auditory methods.

TABLE 3

RELATION OF LEARNING PROCESSES TO ACADEMIC TASKS

ACADEMIC TASK	LEARNING PROCESS
READING	
Stage I - Decoding	Visual perception, memory, sequential memory and/or motor integrative function, fine motor coordination (tactile, kinesthetic, motor coordination)
Stage II - Comprehension	Auditory discrimination, memory, sequential memory, motor integrative function, cognitive abstract skills
SPELLING	
Phonic	Auditory discrimination and auditory sequential memory
Visual	Visual perception, visual sequential memory
WRITING AND DRAWING	Visual-motor integration, fine motor coordination of the hands
WRITTEN ARITHMETIC	Visual perception, right-left discrimination, visual and auditory sequential memory

They also concluded that even though a child has difficulties with visual perception, memory, sequencing, and visual-motor integration, he will eventually learn to read by using his auditory pathway for remediation.

This has been borne out by my own clinical experience. Children with the most severe reading problems seem to be those with serious problems with auditory discrimination and auditory rote sequential memory. On the other hand, children with poor visual skills with good intelligence and auditory skills seem to gain some degree of reading proficiency eventually. They use context clues from the most meager visual clues, i.e., shape of the whole word or identification of first and last letters. Mrs. Alice Jane Whitsell, Director of the Reading and Language Development Clinic, University of California San Francisco Medical Center, has demonstrated this phenomenon by presenting a random list of words from two categories to a child who was unable to recognize any of them until they were listed under two headings, e.g., animal and fruit, at which time he could read all the words.

Stage I of reading takes place when the child begins to develop reading readiness skills in kindergarten or before, and it requires the ability to identify the written symbol, discriminate figure from background, and appreciate its direction, size and shape. Once the symbol is visually perceived, it is stored for recall. This process of learning involves visual memory for the form, shape and internal details of the written symbol. If the symbol has internal details of several parts in sequence, they must also be remembered in their proper order, a process which requires visual sequential memory. Thus, the child must perceive the symbol, store it, recall the sequence of the parts if and when necessary, and then carry out a motor act with a pencil to reproduce the symbol. This latter act represents visual-motor integrative function.

By the time a child reaches or completes kindergarten he is expected to be able to recognize all the letters of the alphabet, associate them with a name, recall them from memory, and take them down in dictation. This final task requires good visual-motor integrative function and an ability to discriminate and recognize the sound and associate it with a letter (the phoneme-grapheme relationship). The decoding process of Stage I is considered to be word calling, whereas Stage II requires comprehension and is dependent on good auditory skills, usually associated with good expressive and receptive language.

HANDWRITING

Problems in handwriting are usually expressions of poor fine motor coordination of the hands and poor visual-motor integrative function. A child may be able to identify the symbol yet be unable to reproduce it. Children with poor visual-motor integrative abilities and poor fine motor coordination of the hands usually have marked difficulty with written school work. Their hands tire with writing and their labored efforts are often illegible. They cannot

do the usual amount of written work and develop a resistance to all writing. Feelings of general discouragement
develop towards school work when copious written work is
expected and when school papers are marked as messy or
unacceptable by the teachers. Handwriting problems alone
can frequently become significant deterrents to a child's
effective adaptation to school and learning.

SPELLING

      Children with serious problems with the visual
pathway for learning in the presence of good auditory skills
and good intelligence can eventually develop some degree
of reading proficiency. They may, however, go on to have
problems with spelling and arithmetic. Spelling difficulties
often reflect profound visual and/or auditory sequential
memory problems and first become apparent when the child
is unable to learn the letters of the alphabet, days of the
week, months of the year in order, and also shows rote
memory problems when counting by two's, three's, etc.
Phonetic spelling requires the ability to discriminate the
sounds within a word and to recall the sounds in the order
heard, while spelling by sight requires a visual memory for
the whole word with an ability to remember the position of
the letters in the order seen. The children with auditory
sequential memory problems also often have difficulty in
following a series of verbal directions and may be accused
by parents and teachers of tuning-out and/or daydreaming.

ARITHMETIC

      Early arithmetic skills involve the same tasks used in
acquiring reading, writing, and spelling, i.e., attentiveness, symbol and sound-symbol recognition, ability to copy
and write symbols from dictation, right-left discrimination,
rote and non-rote visual and auditory sequential memory,
as well as concepts of number, amount, size, body image
and time. Children with difficulty in acquiring arithmetic
skills often show problems with sequential memory, body
image, right-left confusion, and poor directional sense.
These children tend to read from right to left; for example,
they will write 12 for 21, and forget which column of

numbers to add first.   Some children have an inability to
remember the sequential steps necessary for written arithmetic computation.   Poor auditory sequential memory and
associated inattention and distractibility often result in
difficulties with learning the basic combinations, computing
arithmetic orally, and counting by rote (two's, three's,
etc.).   Those children with poor auditory sequential memory
must rely on other existing skills and can sometimes com-
pensate by using laborious methods of writing everything
down, starting at the beginning with each interruption,
counting with fingers, counting marks on the page, or any
available method to experience the process.   (See Table 3.)

3 Natural History of Specific Learning Disorders

Since the child with a specific learning disorder presents normal intelligence, his difficulties with acquired language skills perplex his parents as well as his teachers. Many problems ensue between the child and his parents on the basis of this obscurity, allowing the parents and teachers to make unfounded assumptions by implying motives of laziness, an unwillingness to try, and lack of interest. As part of the confusion, the parents often blame the school and teachers for being ineffective, while the school blames the parents for negligence.

The events that finally lead to an evaluation have often caused serious disruption within the family. The learning problems can cause the family to become dysfunctional, or they can be focused upon by an already dysfunctional family. Professionals see these children and their families in all stages of hope, confusion, despair, blame, and in a search for a simple cause and solution. These sad, angry children and their bewildered, angry parents are usually referred only after a school crisis of academic failure or acting-out behavior has occurred. The crisis has usually followed mounting stress at home and school, and is often expressed by somatic complaints of headaches, gastrointestinal disturbance, or sometimes by enuresis and/or encopresis (Taichert, 1971). Elaborate systems of denial, projection or blame have developed to protect the parents against the serious threats to their own self-esteem. Sometimes conflicts over values and course of management develop between the parents. Sometimes they blame each other for the handicap and often use the myth that "If it weren't for Billy's reading problems, everything would be all right." This myth may serve to direct attention from more serious problems within the family itself.

The parents are often unaware of the child's problems until he enters school. Then he is usually described by his teachers as having a short attention span, difficulty in sitting still, distractibility, poor tolerance for frustration, poor fine or gross motor coordination, inability to follow instructions, and/or a tendency to daydream. This description is a statement of the child's neurophysiological state. The hyperactive, distractible, wandering child is often detected almost immediately after entering school. In some ways, this type of child is fortunate in that he calls attention to himself earlier than the silent, withdrawn, timid child who bothers no one by remaining in his seat daydreaming. Although the parents have been unaware of the child's problems before entering school, a careful history will often reveal a delayed onset of expressive language, clumsiness, hypotonia, variable hyperactivity, irritability, and/or impulsivity.

His first experience of failure at school occurs when he is unable to do what is expected of him and he becomes the target of other children's abuse and is exposed to teasing and name-calling, such as "dumb" and "stupid." These children have great cause for worry in the face of poor coping ability, for they generally have poor impulse control and low tolerance for frustration.

From the beginning, these easily frustrated children achieve independence with difficulty. Their frequent cries of frustration involve the parents and provide little opportunity for the children to learn to delay gratification and for the parents to feel success in helping them to achieve autonomy. These children usually need constant care; they cannot feel the sense of mastery that comes from taking care of their own needs, e.g., dressing themselves, eating without incident, and taking responsibility for their own school work.

When they first enter school, the parents happily assist with the school work but, as the demands at school increase and become unrealistic, these children resist homework; the parents become increasingly anxious and the homework sessions become scenes of heated battle. The responsibility for initiating and doing homework soon shifts from the child to the parents, with the child attempting to avoid the learning tasks and the homework sessions altogether. He begins to sense the parents' vested interest in wanting him to do well. If the family expectations are too great, there is little room for the child to make mistakes; he becomes fearful, often stops trying, and after a while may even stop caring.

Once the responsibility for homework shifts from the child to the parents, they have entered into a power struggle. The child, being in control, will always win, leaving the parents angry and helpless. This problem is often further complicated by the development of a covert power struggle that begins when the parents unwittingly give the child additional power by saying, "You're doing this just to hurt me." The obliging child can become very successful in manipulating his parents through this additional sense of power.

This inappropriate shift in responsibility has a profound effect on the development of family life. While we often think about the normative stages in the development of the individual, little is said about the normative stages of family development. If we stop to look at the effect that childhood learning problems have on the longitudinal development of family life, we can see how such children interfere with this development. The problems can, though not necessarily, begin immediately following birth when the parents begin to adapt to an infant who is hyper- or hypoactive, silent, irritable, slow to develop language function, has coordination problems, poor tolerance for frustration, and/or distractibility.

We will assume that all has gone well with the mother and father alone until the child is born or enters school. The parents have successfully completed their courtship and have assumed the new commitments that go with marriage. They have accomplished this by establishing territorial boundaries between themselves as well as with the extended kin and community through an active selection of friends and relatives. The demands made by their in-laws for visiting and offers for help have been reconciled and steps have been taken gradually to establish independence for success as marriage partners. (Jay Haley, 1970, in a recent talk, discussed the longitudinal development of the family and pointed out the fact that man is the only animal that has in-laws who later become grand-parents.) Upon arrival of the first child, they enter the stage of parenthood in which new demands require adjust-ment of parental roles and values.

The next significant stage of family development occurs when the child leaves home for the first time to enter kindergarten. The success of this separation depends on the child's neurodevelopmental state, his ability to learn and acquire language skills, and the ability of the parents and child to separate from one another. This stage of separation is met with the greatest success when the child's stage of development is in phase with the expec-tations of the school system.

If, however, the child still needs care, i.e., to be dressed, spoken for, or is unable to do any school work alone, an awful dilemma develops. This dilemma is one of the greatest threats to growth and maturity of the child and his family and begins when the responsibility for the child's behavior gradually shifts to the parents. Since the child has difficulty in assuming responsibility for himself as a result of delays in development of good motor coor-dination and problems in acquiring early language skills, the parents begin to assume more and more responsibility for his behavior. The child begins to face tasks at school and at home that he is unable to perform. The gap widens between what is expected of him and what he is actually able to do. When the school and parental expectations are completely out of phase with the child's development, he has little or no opportunity to assume responsibility for himself, never achieves a sense of mastery that comes through personal success, and gradually fails to develop autonomy. In turn, the parents are unable to experience the success and joy that comes from watching their child develop such mastery of skills and independence.

Recently, I observed two children with learning problems in the same family who had trouble gaining inde-pendence. The younger girl had failed to mature, was dependent, fearful, anxious, and lived in a world of fantasy. She made her father feel successful through her dependence and his need to control, whereas he felt extremely unsuccessful with the older daughter who was strong-willed, defiant, non-communicative, and rebellious.

Whenever there is a failure of a child to develop autonomy, the family will experience stress from its unsuccessful attempt to accomplish this important phase of development. The parents and school start playing their game of blame and shame, and indulge themselves in unfounded motivational assumptions--for example, "They don't want to teach him," "He doesn't want to learn." As school work becomes gradually more and more difficult and unrealistic for the child, responsibility for homework and self-care gradually shifts to the mother or father, depending on who assumes the primary role of "mothering." The child blames the mother for the hardship imposed upon him and begins to resist the school work altogether. The homework sessions become emotionally charged and the only time the child approaches the learning task is at the parents' nagging insistence.

Once the parents assume responsibility for the child's behavior, either the mother or father will begin to worry and fear that if the homework sessions are not initiated by them the work will never get done. In fact, the work never does get done because the child is incapable of meeting their expectations.

The child and parents have experienced considerable sadness by the time they are seen for an evaluation. They have had an ongoing unsuccessful relationship with each other and the child has been unable to separate from his parents with any degree of comfort or success. As a result, this normative stage of family life is unsuccessfully completed and the parents have difficulty returning to their original functional diad state (mother and father alone) and may continue as a dysfunctional triad instead.

The aforementioned process may be one phenomenological description of "passive-resistant behavior" and childhood depression.

4   The Family and Communication

The Origin of the Family

The origin of each family is based on early complementary roles established between husband and wife which formed the basis of their selection of one another at the time of marriage. For example, the wife may have agreed to be a dependent, helpless housewife so that her husband could become the aggressive, independent provider, or each may have agreed to look after him- or herself without dependency on the other. The husband and wife become natural or adoptive parents on the arrival of their first newborn or on selection of an adopted child. The child is assigned a role, determined by the parents' value system, complementary role assignment, and position of power within the family group. The family is functional when each adult role complements the other (Speigel, 1957) and when the child (or children) assumes an appropriate role, determined by the parents' complementarity. The child's role is also determined by genetic sexuality, sibling position in the family, and physical and intellectual endowment.

Each member within the family serves a function to maintain the concept of "family homeostasis" introduced by Jackson (1957), i.e., the interplay of dynamic forces which tend to maintain equilibrium among family members. When the expectation level is too high, the complementary roles fail and adjustment is required for restoration of function. The equilibrium within the family is facilitated by the transaction of roles (Speigel, 1957). If this fails, the parents begin to assign inappropriate roles to their children such as rescuer, pacifier, worrier, trouble-maker, failure, etc., in order to restore or maintain equilibrium. When one or more family members experience stress from this inappropriate role assignment, the family may be considered dysfunctional. In addition to the complementary roles and position of power of the parents within the family, the value the parents place on achievement, gender and physical appearance determine, to a great extent, the child's role within the family. The child who threatens the parents' value system becomes the focus of attention for family conflict and dysfunction.

Myth. Ferreira (1963) discusses the functional importance of the family myth in maintaining homeostatic mechanisms in family life. He defines the term "family myth" as a series of fairly well integrated beliefs shared by all members of the family concerning each other, their mutual position in the family, and beliefs that go unchallenged by everyone involved in spite of reality distortions. The family image is not necessarily the myth, but a front to cover up for the inner image of the group to which all family members contribute and which they apparently strive to preserve. Help is usually sought whenever some important family myth becomes inoperative or is seriously threatened by developing events. The search for help may be the last attempt to maintain the status quo and reestablish the previously steady state. The therapist is often expected to help the family regain the formula and to maintain the myth (Gehrke and Kirschenbaum, 1967).

When there is a theme of happiness, there is a tendency to maintain the status quo by doing nothing or by obstructing any action in psychotherapy, whereas the theme of unhappiness asks for help and is aimed at promoting action, i.e., doing something about improving the situation. Although the unhappiness theme asks for help, the family still hopes to maintain the myth that "everything would be fine if it weren't for his stealing" and the psychotherapist must be careful not to become an integral part of this family myth. In contrast, the family theme of happiness asks the psychotherapist to strengthen the myth that all is well and that there is no need for worry.

Most family myths have their origin in the early days of the relationship, i.e., during courtship and the first two or three years of marriage when contracts for togetherness are established around complementary roles (Ferreira,

1963). The myth describes roles and behavior which, in turn, strengthen and consolidate these roles. The myth is called into play whenever certain tensions threaten to disrupt ongoing relationships. When a baby is planned or a decision for an adoption occurs, the myth that "everything will be fine when the baby comes" may hope to solve the problems of marital distress. The myth is to the relationship what the defense is to the individual, i.e., it acts as a safety valve with a survival value. A lack of insight is necessary to distort reality and to maintain oneself within a given myth.

In the case to be presented the family myth or inner image of happiness was also reflected in their outer image of happy togetherness. Family happiness was an insightless belief shared and maintained by all family members, including the identified patient whom the parents were unable to accept as handicapped. Each had to protect the other from accepting the existence of neurodevelopmental problems, for each felt the other was incapable of tolerating this disappointment and sadness. Since they chose to believe that they were happy and their son, Alan, had no real problem, all help was resisted. Alan only needed to try harder, even though the school had placed him on a half-day program because they were unable to cope with his acting-out behavior in a regular program.

A case demonstrating a happiness theme and myth that sadness is intolerable

Family M.: Alan, a 13 year old was the youngest of three children. He was referred by his school for evaluation and management of his learning and behavior problems. The referral was prompted by failing grades in mathematics and geography, poor handwriting and spelling skills, and unsuccessful peer and teacher relationships. His school counselor and parents shared the same view, i.e., if he was properly motivated, he could do better. The school blamed the parents and the parents blamed the school for his poor performance.

Alan was a very tall, robust, early

pubescent boy with beginning voice change and acne who exchanged anxious smiles with his mother, and smiled and laughed with both parents throughout the initial interview, particularly when a serious or grave issue was discussed. He talked incessantly when given the opportunity in an intense, shrill, monotonous voice, furtively glancing from one parent to the other, seeking constant support and approval from their smiling faces, their rationalization and excuse-making. This happy, good-natured "togetherness" was exhausting to observe. Initially, it stimulated the smiling response from the therapist. However, it soon became apparent that each family member had the responsibility to keep the others happy, in a rescue attempt to prevent intolerable sadness. The mother laughed with tears in her eyes and the father laughed with a facial tick easily mistaken for a wink of the eye. Later, each parent (in an attempt to spare each other's feelings) discussed in the absence of the other the fears and disappointments that came from a realistic view of their son's "hopeless" handicap. Each felt that the other was incapable of tolerating sadness.

The family's need to rationalize, deny feelings, and keep each other happy prevented a realistic view of Alan. Each report card period became a catastrophic event. Alan failed to bring home warnings of impending failure and signed his father's name to his own report card to protect himself and his family from learning of his school failure. His father accused him of deceit and dishonesty and his mother immediately came to his defense and protection. The parents tended to blame Alan for not trying, assuming he could do better work, and blamed the school for their poor teaching methods.

In the absence of his wife, Mr. M. expressed his discomfort in not experiencing

the "normal" expected feelings of love and
giving towards his dependent wife and handicapped son whom he feared would need support
for the rest of his life. Mr. M. as a young
boy had to fend for himself and did not have
the opportunity to "receive" from anyone. He
was bothered by his wife's interest in togetherness, had an aversion to children and, since a
forced semiretirement following an illness, he
could barely tolerate the closeness of the
interpersonal family relationships. He disliked
family gatherings, had many acquaintances but
had not wanted any close friendships with
people. He detested emotionalism and displays
of temper, as well as extreme hilarity and/or
horseplay.

The parents were married before completing their formal education, however, they
had worked together successfully in achieving
considerable economic success.

Alan was born weighing 6 pounds 12
ounces following a short, induced, precipitous
labor and was described by his mother as a
"battered baby." He had cephalohematomas,
depression of the left parietal area, ecchymoses
of the eyes, and neonatal distress which
required two days of incubator care. He went
home on the fifth day of life with a good
sucking reflex and no problems in feeding. He
was a good baby in the newborn period and
rocked in his crib as an older infant. He
walked late, had poor coordination and tended
to fall and stumble. He startled easily and
had an intolerance to loud noises. Toilet
training was accomplished without difficulty.

Alan's language development began at the
usual time, but his speech was of poor quality
and sparse quantity. At the time of evaluation,
his speech was characterized by poor sound
formations, immature automatic grammatical
usage, and his voice had an intense, harsh,

monotonous quality. Alan spoke incessantly, justifying his problems or his behavior by the use of denial of feelings, excuses and rationalization. He said, "I am dominated by both hands." He wrote with his right hand and ate with his left. His drawing of a man was started at the bottom of the page and worked upward. He had difficulty with tying his shoes and buttoning his clothes as a small youngster and had problems with drawing, writing and coloring since entering school. The first grade was repeated, due to "immaturity," i.e., poor pencil grip, hyperactivity, short attention span, and an inability to write the letters even though he reportedly began to read before entering school. Alan read at grade level, but had increasing difficulty with mathematics, spelling, and geography.

Alan thought of himself as different and poorly formed. He experienced feelings of worthlessness, reinforced by his increasing difficulty with all written school work, i.e., handwriting, arithmetic, and reports. His problems in arithmetic demonstrated errors in lining up numbers in columns and recalling the sequential steps necessary for written computation.

Findings on neurological examination were consistent with the diagnosis of neurodevelopmental dysfunction, as evidenced by fine and gross intention tremors and incoordination of both hands, disturbance of balance, problems with directional sense and distance, difficulty with concepts of size and amount, and extremely poor body image.

The developmental assessment found Alan to have normal intelligence on the Wechsler Intelligence Scale for Children (WISC); his Performance I.Q. was 97, Verbal I.Q. 120, with a Full Scale I.Q. of 110. On tests of visual-motor integrative function, he performed like a much younger child.

In the speech and language evaluation he showed marked difficulty with the visual and auditory sequential memory tasks of the Illinois Test of Psycholinguistic Abilities (ITPA). He demonstrated problems with the quality of his spontaneous expressive language and inability to repeat on immediate recall either meaningful or non-meaningful multisyllabic words.

The educational evaluation included parts of the Durrell Analysis of Reading Difficulty, Space Reading Diagnostic Scale, Gates-McKillop Diagnostic Reading Test, Monroe Reading Aptitude Test, and Spencer Sentence Memory Test. Alan could read and comprehend at or above grade level. The test for visual memory for forms, however, gave him an age equivalent of 4 years 5 months. Throughout the educational evaluation, Alan in a running commentary said that he could do better other times and other places. His handwriting was noted as labored and his grip was unusual. He performed like a 9-1/2-year-old boy on the sentence memory test.

Tests of vision and hearing were within normal limits and the electroencephalogram was read as normal for his age.

In summary, 13-year-old Alan, a junior high school youngster with normal intelligence, had difficulty in specific learning processes, i.e., visual memory for forms, visual-motor integrative function, and visual and auditory sequential memory, associated with poor fine motor coordination of the hands, poor body image and balance, confused directional sense, and poor concepts of time and amount. Alan read at grade level, but had marked difficulty with mathematics and handwriting, extremely poor self-esteem, and anxiety resulting from a poor manner of coping in the family by denying

feelings, making excuses and inappropriate
affect. The "family rule" that each person was
responsible for the other's happiness could be
characterized as "happiness at all cost,"
"whistling in the dark," "crying on the inside
and laughing on the outside." Recommendations
for Alan included a special academic program,
family therapy, and trial on medication for
hyperactivity, distractibility, and inattentiveness.

This family had an outward appearance of happiness
shown by smiling faces, statements of optimism, denial of
sadness, excessive excuse-making and rationalization.
Although Alan, the son and identified patient, was
struggling at school with learning problems, neither he nor
his parents could accept the fact that there were real
neurodevelopmental problems in learning. Each parent felt
the other could not accept the realization of this handicap
and each felt the other was incapable of tolerating sadness. As hard as the child tried, the parents felt he
wasn't trying hard enough, or else that the problem was
really with the school. Everyone worked hard at keeping
himself and everyone else happy; no one was allowed to
be sad because "sadness is intolerable." Although happiness was the general theme and principal myth, the idea
that no one could tolerate sadness permitted this family to
function as they did. In an early contract between the
parents, each had assumed responsibility for the other's
happiness. The mother's happiness was to come from
homemaking, i.e., being a good mother and wife, with the
father making all the decisions, being the provider and
assuming responsibility for his wife's happiness.

Scapegoat. While the myth is considered to be a
defense mechanism to maintain homeostasis within the
family system, an emotionally disturbed child can often
become a scapegoat to maintain that myth, i.e., "everything would be fine if it weren't for his lying, bedwetting,
school failure, stealing, fire-starting, etc." The deviant
or scapegoat within a group performs a valuable function
by channeling group tensions and providing a basis for
family solidarity (Bell and Vogel, 1968a).

Vogel and Bell's (1968a) study of emotionally disturbed children acting as scapegoats showed that the child with a learning problem can be induced into this role by threatening the family value system, and thereby represents a symbol of failure. Therefore, whenever a child with a learning or behavior problem is the identified patient, the problem of scapegoating must be considered. While the family achieves unity through the scapegoat and gives the child sufficient support to maintain his role in the family, the use of him as a scapegoat is often incompatible with equipping the child to maintain an adjustment outside of the nuclear family.

In short, the scapegoating mechanism is functional for the family as a group but is dysfunctional for the emotional health of the child and for his adjustment outside the family orientation. The family prefers to scapegoat its own child when the ties with the community are tenuous or when their acceptance and own self-exteem are in jeopardy. The child is in a helpless position; the cost to him is high in relation to the functional gains of the family. The parents rationalize their behavior by defining themselves as the victims. The scapegoating serves as a personality stabilizing process by allowing the parents to project their own difficulties onto their children. The child who is dubbed as a school failure or bedwetter can function at home, but not outside the family system.

Scapegoating of the neurodevelopmentally handicapped child. Two examples of scapegoating are presented in which the children had learning and behavior problems which threatened the family value system and self-esteem of the parents. In the first case the family had been made dysfunctional by a hyperactive, impulsive, angry boy. The parents felt sufficiently victimized to seek help through this child who was allowed to tyrannize them through his role as the "bad" boy. They showed a marked resistance to therapy in an attempt to maintain the status quo and protect their privacy. In the second case the child channeled attention from the problems of distance and lack of communication that already existed between the parents.

Family D.: Roger, an 11-year 3-month-old second adopted child of professional parents, was referred for evaluation of his learning and behavior problems. The parents were experiencing feelings of anger and helplessness as a result of his low frustration tolerance, impulsivity, and frequent outbursts of rage at home and at school.

Roger weighed 14 pounds when he was adopted at 2 months of age, was difficult to feed, and presented problems in care from the first day--he was irritable, whiny, and nothing seemed to satisfy him. The parents took turns rocking him and often all three ended up sipping wine. Roger's motor development was quite precocious and he had excellent large motor skills. His language development was delayed in onset, and the quality and quantity of his speech was described as poor. Roger repeated the first grade because of immaturity, hyperactivity, and an inability to master reading-readiness skills. Towards the end of the third grade he finally learned to say all the letters of the alphabet in order. At the time of evaluation he had been identified by the school as an educationally handicapped child and was receiving special reading instruction a half-hour each day and private reading therapy for one hour a week.

On educational evaluation, he was found to be 3 years behind his chronological age in grade level in most areas of school achievement. He had better auditory than visual skills for learning and demonstrated marked difficulties with visual memory for words and forms.

The developmental assessment showed him to be of normal intelligence (Full Scale I.Q. of 109 on the WISC). His greatest strength was in number manipulation and his most marked difficulty was on vocabulary test items. On

projective tests he had an unusual amount of
hostile, murderous fantasies; 4 out of 5 of the
Thematic Apperception Test stories dealt with
killings, directed especially toward male
figures. His drawings and those of the family
dealt with violence and an interest in guns
and knives.

Roger wore long bangs to cover his face.
He was very self-conscious, unable to talk
about his feelings, restless, impulsive and
avoided eye contact. Except for slight
difficulties in fine motor coordination of the
hands, the neurological examination was
essentially negative.

The initial family interview was intensely
disturbing for the family. Roger had been
moody and difficult in the car for a long
2-1/2-hour drive to the city. He resented
being brought in as the "bad" boy and had
considerable concern about his image. He
tried to hide his feelings, although he
repeatedly offered the information that there
was "nothing wrong with him." Mrs. D.
described her resentment and poor health as
due to Roger's unmanageable behavior.
Throughout the interview, Roger registered disgust and ridicule of those about him, either
through imitation or mockery. He responded to
many questions, whether directed to him or
not, with "It's none of your business." When
asked what he knew about his adoption, he
fled from the office to the street. At this time
and at others, he expressed the family's
reluctance to want to talk about themselves.

Mr. D. was a remote but affable,
personable man who had a slight handicap
since early childhood. He handled his feelings
at a distance by joking and teasing, but
showed an honest, sympathetic concern for his
son and wife. Great demands at work had kept
him from his family until the previous year

when he was forced to take a leave and stay home to help his wife with the burden of child care when she was confined to bed with migraine headaches and ulcer pain. Mrs. D., a tall, well-educated, good-looking woman, with dark circles under her eyes, appeared chronically ill. She had no success in setting limits for this extremely active boy. Periods of quiet and calm were reached only after she resorted to angry beatings which she felt Roger initiated. She was very uncomfortable with her feelings of anger and fear of losing control.

Both parents grew up during the depression in rural America where they worked hard for what they had--Mrs. D. said they weren't given "everything" like their children. She complained about never having a sense of completion with the task of housework and child rearing. Until the children arrived, her life was orderly and dependable. She wanted her house to be immaculate and felt she was judged as a failure if her children weren't successful or her house was dirty. She had very low self-esteem and her unsuccessful, handicapped son constantly threatened her effectiveness and competence as an adult.

The parents demonstrated the "adopted parents' syndrome," i.e., in order to prove their love, they worked to achieve happiness at all cost. They tended to give into Roger's constant demands. Thus, the parents were faced with the tyranny of a boy who had begun to dominate the family with bribery and threats. The parents' inability to set limits combined with Roger's short attention span and poor frustration tolerance, had not allowed him to develop adequate impulse control. Roger had an interest in powerful, fast-moving vehicles and showed a keen interest in instant joy and thrills, and demonstrated through <u>body language</u> what he was unable to express in words. Both parents enjoyed talking about his dare-devil, risk-taking activities. Roger obligingly acted as the "beast" according to the mother's predictions, while the father seemed to encourage this behavior with his amusement and tendency to stay uninvolved.

Roger appeared to have a specific learning disorder and was expressing severe psychological stress in a family which had become dysfunctional. The recommendations were: 1) family therapy, 2) a trial on medication (Ritalin^R 5 to 10 mg. bid.), and 3) a private school which would provide small classes and a therapeutic educational setting.

Change in the family system occurred almost immediately following the evaluation when change occurred in Roger's behavior through a favorable response to medication. Roger's impulsivity and short attention span improved on Ritalin^R 10 mg. bid. He became more responsive to management. During several stormy months of family therapy, the family resisted change and resented talking about their feelings. At first, they allowed Roger to act as family spokesman and attack the therapist verbally; however, once this was stopped, the focus began to shift from the child, who had been viewed as the culprit, to the parents. The family began to see Roger as an extremely sensitive, handicapped child who cared about his feelings and those of others. His poor language skills interfered with his ability to express himself openly, accounting in part for his acting-out behavior. His reading began to improve, after he met with a tutor without objection. Mrs. D. was given support and was relieved of blame. She learned not to be so hard on herself and began using her good intelligence and talents in interests outside of the home. Her migraine headaches and ulcer pains improved gradually.

In the next family the mother and child both felt victimized; however, the mother wanted to keep the child as he was, which prevented her from looking at the poor relationship she had with her husband and with her own problems with sexual identity. When the child experienced a crisis outside the family in relationships with peers and teachers at school he was moved from one school to another for temporary relief.

> Family B.: Randy B. was a third grade 9-year-old adopted child. He was the younger of three children, referred by his school because of difficulty with periods of uncontrollable rage, easy distractibility, poor impulse control, inability to play with peers, and repeated suspension for this behavior.

> Randy was adopted at 4 weeks of age and was considered to be jaundiced through the fifth week of life. He was late in walking, talking and acquiring fine and gross motor coordination skills. He was a very irritable baby who startled easily and no amount of soothing seemed to satisfy him. Feeding was described as the "battle of the bottle," since he continued to prefer the bottle and refused to eat from a spoon. Randy was not walking without support until 24 months of age. As he became older, his poor balance and coordination delayed the onset of bicycle riding. He was late in developing expressive language, but spoke in full sentences once he began to talk.

> Randy had difficulty in acquiring reading and writing skills and was somewhat behind his grade level and chronological age in achievement. At school he was distractible, impulsive and had inappropriate behavior for peer success. He appeared to be either over- or under-controlled. His incoordination and mild choreoathetoid movements had been interpreted by the teachers and neighbors as a swaggering feminine gait. Mrs. B. was vague about their

previous professional consultations although various specialists had recommended medication for his hyperactivity.

On neurological examination he demonstrated marked dyspraxia of the upper and lower extremities, with flailing motions of the arms and hands on rapid alternating movements, worse on the left than right, poor fine motor coordination of the hands, better on the right, disturbance of balance, dystonic posturing on tandem walking, extremely hyperactive deep tendon reflexes, positive toe signs on the left, and left ankle clonus. These findings were consistent with a diagnosis of moderate to severe neurodevelopmental dysfunction. His drawings and handwriting were labored, and his drawing of a person appeared feminine or bisexual. His "3 wishes" were: 1) to dress up and look nice when he goes to school, 2) to have a beautiful limousine with a chauffeur, and 3) to have all the Safeways in the world so he could eat all the candy he wanted. On each visit Randy expressed an interest in the examiner's shoes, and his mother delighted in commenting on his interest in women's clothing.

The developmental assessment and the educational evaluation showed evidence of a specific learning disability. Randy had test scores of normal intelligence on the WISC, with marked disabilities in learning processes which involved visual-motor integration and auditory sequential memory.

Both parents were Ivy League graduates, flawlessly groomed, affluent and well-bred. Mrs. B. recalled her own childhood with sadness; she was the less-favored daughter and was considered the ugly duckling. She described her own parents as strict and controlling, which accounted for her own child rearing attitudes and her strong disapproval of the "over-permissiveness of today's parents."

The family interview demonstrated the parents' anger with one another. Even though Mrs. B. was angry with her husband for arriving late, both parents tried to maintain a sense of propriety and control.

Mr. B. was a slight, balding man with small features, who sat in a chair against the wall apart from everyone. He was dressed impeccably in a pin-striped suit, and kept his arms and legs neatly crossed. He tolerated the interview in a strained, disdainful manner and made it clear that he was a "busy man" with little time for "this kind of business." In an attempt to direct the conversation, he frequently said, "Well, that subject has been covered."

Mrs. B. was an attractive, distraught, slender, angular woman with short hair, dressed expensively in understated, tailored attire. She spoke in a tense, high-pitched voice and tried to avoid discussion of her feelings of anger and resentment. She vacillated between denial of feelings and a demonstration of great insight and display of feelings.

Randy was dressed beautifully in a spotless outfit and sat quietly with a wistful face, twiddling his thumbs throughout the interview. With an angelic face, he constantly looked to his mother's face for approval or disapproval. He never spoke spontaneously, and it was hard to imagine that this pretty, noncommittal boy could be the demon described by the parents and school.

Randy heard his mother describe him as a child who could not be trusted, who lied, cheated, stole and "frankly is without a conscience," all the while justifying her anger and punitive restrictions. It soon became apparent that Mrs. B. tended to disqualify or invalidate Randy's feelings and thoughts, i.e., "You don't really feel this way or mean what you say." In one breath Mrs. B. predicted evil, showed self-pity and denied feelings. Randy was described as "all ears," a "peeping Tom" and an eavesdropper on adult conversations. Since Randy was not to be trusted, he was denied play because he was destructive, friendships because he didn't know how to play with other children, candy because it was not good for his orthodontic appliance (he was accused of stealing candy), or access to the icebox to help himself because "He is fed adequate, nourishing, healthy food at mealtime and no 9-year-old boy should have free reign of eating from the icebox at any time." Pencils, crayons and scissors were withheld until a year ago because "He would mark up the walls." His transgressions were often brought to the parents' attention by a "perfect" sister who did no wrong. He had recently signed a pact with his father which would deny everything if he transgressed again, including stripping his room bare for an undetermined length of time. Several times both parents expressed pride in his ability to behave like a gentleman when they were out to dinner.

Although Mr. B. accused his wife of being too severe a disciplinarian, he left it up to her because he was seldom home. He was often called away on business trips and spent little time with the family; sometimes when he was out late with clients he stayed away all night.

Randy was found to have a neurodevelopmental disorder expressed as a specific learning disability, associated with difficulty with balance, coordination, impulsivity, and distractibility. He demonstrated serious symptoms of psychological stress and confusion with gender role, symptoms which were necessary to function in this already dysfunctional family. The restrictive environment plus Randy's wish to please, guaranteed the mother's prediction of the "bad child." His symptoms permitted the parents to focus on him, and to distance themselves from their own problems and from each other. Randy had trouble developing inner control, since all control seemed to come from without. He was clearly confused about his gender role. He frequently referred to himself as a girl.

Family therapy, a trial on medication, and special academic consideration were recommended. Both parents resisted the idea of family therapy and medication. Randy studied with a home teacher while the family looked for another school setting.

Patterns of Communication

A discussion will be presented to demonstrate the way in which patterns of communication maintain inappropriate roles and family dysfunction.

Closed family system. A closed family system is one in which the child continually receives double-level messages (Satir, 1964) from parents who do not allow the child to question the disparity of communication. This places pressures of a vise-like quality or double-bind on the child, so that when he obeys on one level of meaning he is disobeying on another; thus, his behavior continuously invites parental rejection. This child "has been had"--he's damned if he does and damned if he doesn't. (See Family B., page 36.)

In this system, secretiveness, deceit and covert behavior are encouraged because the child is made to feel that there is no way out, he dare not lose or ever be bad, and average is not good enough. In this kind of family the possibility for direct open expression is not permitted, the environment allows for no mistakes, and punishment is

often unreasonable. The child is left with dismal alterna-
tives, i.e., obsessive fear of failure, deceit, anti-social
behavior, or the attitude of not caring. The neurologically
handicapped child, i.e., the child with a specific learning
disorder, who lives in a closed family system becomes the
identified patient in an already dysfunctional family not
only because of his handicap but because of the expression of symptoms necessary to exist within this kind of
family. As Virginia Satir (1964) states:

> "A child's deviant behavior can be functional
> behavior within a dysfunctional family system.
> . . . it's this child who holds the power to
> make or break the magic circle of family
> balance . . . . the homeostatic system which
> includes an identified patient can remain rela-
> tively stable for a long time [p. 38]."

The labeling of such a child as disturbed, schizoid, psy-
chotic, autistic, or mentally retarded only helps to maintain the system at first, and encourages the parents to
maintain their own defenses of rationalization and projection. The neurologically handicapped child thus becomes
the patient not only because of his neurological dysfunction but because his difficulties are used in a conflict
between the parents which results in mutual lowering of
their self-esteem.

   Interactional patterns of communication in a dysfunctional family. As we have already learned, the family
myth is an insightless idea and distortion of reality shared
by all members of the family. When this idea is brought
into play it acts as a mechanism to maintain family
homeostasis. The family chosen for discussion demonstrates the way in which patterns of communication reflect
the myth and maintain the homeostasis. The mother has
the belief that success in anything is achieved through a
"balance" implying a debt or that a good act will offset
a bad one. Once a balance is achieved "everything will
be fine." This idea is not only a distortion of reality
but it requires a task that can never be achieved. No
one, therefore, ever feels successful, especially Mary,
their daughter with learning and language problems. In
this way the mother continuously reinforces the idea that

her children let her down. Their failure to succeed invites her criticism and her disillusionment evokes their feelings of guilt.

When the family was seen together, the basic pattern of communication involved shame and blame opposed by defensiveness and counter-blame between two people. A third person would then protect and ally himself with the last person attacked through the use of an attack with an irrelevant statement. This shift in alliance prevented the resolution of any meaningful transaction and, therefore, helped maintain the status quo.

The shift in alliance was very difficult to handle for it served as an effective obstruction to change or movement in therapy.

Family G.: Mary, a beautiful 13-year-old, physically mature girl had increasing trouble with school attendance, failure to achieve, extreme sadness, and repeated threats and unsuccessful attempts of running away from home. Her parents were adamant about "the wrong friends" she kept and her interest in boys of other ethnic groups "who show precocious sexual interest and will eventually get her into trouble." She, in turn, had become very defensive in response to her parents' outspoken criticism of her friends. She was encouraged to meet them on the sly, was caught and then accused of sneakiness. These friends were from the integrated school she attended and were unlike the achieving, well-to-do children in her immediate neighborhood, for whom she was disdainful. Mary experienced outrage whenever her mother referred to the "right" children, the importance of learning the "right" things, and keeping "things" balanced.

On psychological testing, Mary had a score of 95 on the verbal tests of the WISC and a performance score of 120, a history of serious reading problems and was entering the eighth grade with a fourth grade reading comprehension. She had a misleading ability to "word call" or decode at the eighth grade level; however, she was unable to comprehend what was read. Her arithmetic skills were four years behind grade level.

The father was a handsome, successful, professional man, an effectual, direct and quick-acting person in his work and an ineffectual, quick-tempered and angry father at home. He grew up in a family where nice people controlled their feelings. He was uncomfortable with his own feelings of anger and those of others. He told his daughter, "You cry all of the time when you're not really sad--you just cry to get attention."

Mrs. G. grew up in South America as an only child without a father. Her mother let her do as she pleased, though she longed for direction and supervision. She said, "If my mother had ever told me what to do I would have known that she cared about me."

The parents came alone for the first interview, even though the mother was clearly instructed to bring Mary with them. They were experiencing feelings of desperate helplessness and bewilderment and seemed to support one another without any apparent discrepancy in values. They shared the same complaints and seemed to make excuses for each other. Mary was seen alone with her parents in the second interview.

On the third visit the oldest daughter, aged 15, was present. Although she had not had trouble with learning, she appeared quarrelsome and surly. She hated school, was generally unhappy, disagreeable, rebellious and hateful with her parents. During the interview she attacked one or the other parent with a disgusted look or an irrelevant statement, to which they found themselves hopelessly responding with statements of accountability.

An example of the conversation with the four family members together, mother, father, Mary the identified patient, and Jane the oldest daughter, is presented.

Mother (directed as a complaint to no one in particular): I'd like the children to spend more time at home. I wish they'd like to be at home. I wish they liked me. I wish the girls would help with the housework. (Although Mary was found to have superior performance skills, poor verbal skills, and a great ability to work with her hands, her mother had not taught her how to sew, cook or do anything where she might feel successful.)

Mary (hopelessly): I'd like to learn to cook but you complain about the way I do things in the kitchen.

Mother (complaining): I wish you girls would clean up your rooms. (irrelevant)

Mary (defensively): I clean my room.

Jane (directed to mother in a disdainful way): Your clean isn't my idea of clean. (attack and alliance with Mary)

Father (directed to Jane): I want your bed made; it really upsets me when your bed isn't made. (emphatic demand)

Jane (directed to father): I would, but you don't get me up early enough in the morning. (blame)

Mary (directed to father): Why should she have to make her bed? You don't make your bed in the morning. (alliance with Jane and attack)

Mother (directed to Jane apologetically, backing

off from her previous wish that she would like help with the housework): You don't have to make the bed all the time, dear, and it needn't be perfect.

At the time this conversation took place, the family was facing a crisis. They wanted Mary to transfer to a new school where she might have a chance to feel more successful. Mary was saying, "The only reason you want me to change schools is because you don't like my friends. I refuse to go to another school." Both parents felt they were about to meet with failure and were desperate with their helplessness. They had never felt that they had any control over their children.

The shifting alliances of the children against the parents and the alliance of the mother and children against the father was one way to obstruct the transaction or completion of any idea, thought or process. It seemed that the mother pulled the rug out from under the father whenever they needed to act together from a position of strength. The mother continually gave into Mary's threats of "I won't love you--I don't like living with you--I'm going to run away from home," for fear of being unloved. The father responded with panic, fearing further loss of control. His raised voice and vehement, harsh stands were made meaningless by the rage and defiant response provoked in his children. His response to their tears and frustration was one of anger and denouncement. The mother felt that she had lost her children. Her attempts to bring them closer through the use of blame and shame merely aroused their anger and hate for which they were then criticized. The mother desperately hoped to achieve a "balance" through her reproach. She reminded them of the ways they misbehaved in the past. She stated hopelessly that the "girls" always let her down and hoped the "girls" would learn something from their past transgressions. She wanted them to do things that were good for them, i.e., eat the right food, read the right books, and attend the right cultural functions, in order to become responsible adults in the future. Her response to the girls' request to see the current movie "MASH" was, "You don't deserve to see it after the way you have acted.   I'd let you go if you would 'balance' it with something good, like an attendance at the opera or a visit to the library." The mother felt that movies like this were not good for their minds, were unintellectual, and would give them bad ideas. Jane said, "Why do you say, 'No, you can't go to the movies' when you know I'll go anyway?"

The family's value system left little room for a youngster with learning problems.   Mary was placed in a helpless position and her only way out was to run away. Their communication style involved the alternative use of blame, shame, and irrelevance.   Their shifting alliances helped to protect one another from change, thus maintaining the status quo.

<u>Parental attitudes and conflicts expressed as disturbed behavior in children.</u>   Delinquent or antisocial childhood behavior is made possible by patterns of verbal and non-verbal communication within the family.   Unresolved, anti-social parental attitudes and conflicts are frequently observed in the antisocial acting-out behavior of children.

Since the early psychoanalytic interest in antisocial acting-out, collaborative studies have continued   (Griffin, Johnson, & Litton, 1968; Johnson & Szurek, 1952; Szurek, 1942).   From these initial studies emerged the thesis that antisocial acting-out in a child is unconsciously initiated, fostered, and sanctioned by the parents, who vicariously achieve gratification of their own poorly integrated, forbid-den impulses through the child's acting out.   Bell and Vogel's (1968a) research with families with a disturbed child acting as a family scapegoat examined this phenomenon in terms of family process and interactional patterns of com-munication.   They found the emotionally disturbed child an embodiment of certain types of conflicts with and between the parents.

These children are given subtle encouragement and permission for disturbed behavior through parental incon-sistency in their expectations and limit-setting, failure to follow through on threats, delayed punishment, and dis-crepancies in communication.   The antisocial behavior in these cases is used in the scapegoating process when the child is both implicitly and explicitly criticized in the persistence of the disturbed behavior. The primary function of scapegoating not only permits the family to maintain its solidarity but also allows one parent to express hostility to the other without directly endangering the marital relationship and permits a child to express a parent's own unresolved, antisocial conflicts.

The two cases that will be discussed have been selected to demonstrate a phenomenological description in terms of family process--how patterns of communication help establish and maintain disturbed and antisocial behavior in children. The aggressive antisocial behavior in the children is a reflection of the parental attitudes and conflicts (Bell & Vogel, 1968a; Gehrke & Kirschenbaum, 1967; Satir, 1964). In these families the parents were unable to openly communicate their differences and feelings of anger and sadness toward one another. The children were induced and encouraged to express a parent's hostile and aggressive attitude, either towards the other parent or toward society on the whole. These families also demonstrate how the parents' own model for assuming responsibility for behavior is assumed by the entire family. Ideally, the responsibility for behavior should be assumed by each person for himself.

In the first of the two families, each person held the other either directly or indirectly responsible for all his sadness and misfortune. Criticism and blame came directly from the other family members. Each person blamed the other in the commonly practiced "blame game," a game successfully practiced as long as someone is willing to accept the blame with a "yes, but" answer. In the second family, the disturbed child was being scrutinized by a powerful, judgmental force or idea outside the family system. Each person held an omnipotent force, i.e., God and the Devil, outside himself responsible for his behavior, allowing the family members to become blameless, easily led, unaccountable creatures who were never held responsible for anything they did.

Responsibility for behavior given to other family members

Family W.: Mrs. W. had just discontinued individual private therapy at the time of her first visit when she brought the "family" in to see if her children and family had been damaged by her serious depression six months earlier. Both parents appeared unusually agreeable, low-keyed and compatible. One wondered why they were seeking help in the face of their "awareness and good judgment." The parents expressed no differences of opinion and the mother spoke for the family in a somewhat detached, well-modulated voice, qualifying everything she said with "sort of" and "kind of," as a way to avoid hurting people's feelings. Whenever she spoke she prefaced her remarks apologetically with "May I say this or that?" asking permission to speak. Her complaints were expressed in collective general references, using "we," "a person," "the family," "you," "one," and never "I." This made her messages unclear, for it was impossible to know about whom she was talking. On the one hand, the mother asked if she was responsible for the family's problems and, on the other hand, she said, "Everything would be fine if our son would stop picking on his sister. The fighting has helped to drive me crazy."

Their daughter, Jean, had developed an involuntary behavior mannerism and their son, Erik, was demonstrating acting-out behavior at school.

During the first interview, their 9-year-old daughter, Jean, crawled on the floor while neither parent either corrected her or asked her to sit in a chair. Their 12-year-old son, Erik, said to both parents, "Why don't you ask her to get off the floor? She's disgusting." He then began to correct his sister and attack his parents for not assuming this unpleasant role themselves. The children began to argue and bicker, each blaming the other with "yes, but look at what you have done to me." The blame and counterblame took on a dissonant tone and rhythm which served as continuous background static. This activity predictably occurred whenever the parents appeared to talk seriously between themselves. Their fighting was induced, encouraged and criticized by both parents. Erik was told by his father that Jean's manners were none of his business and Mrs. W. said with a smiling face, "I can't stand your fighting with Jean. You're always picking on her."

Mrs. W. disliked keeping up her own appearances. She permitted her daughter to act unladylike which reflected and supported her own feelings that it wasn't important to look pretty. Mrs. W. resented her husband's criticism of her appearance. She felt that "If you really cared enough about me you would accept me the way I am." As Mrs. W. allowed Jean to eat with her hands, crawl on the floor and wear her hair in her face, Mr. W. permitted Erik to criticize, ridicule and taunt his sister for this unladylike behavior. Erik was criticized for the role he had assumed to correct his sister and was then accused of fighting.

Erik was openly cruel in his denouncement of Jean. He found her repulsive and wished she were dead. She embarrassed him with his friends and he blamed her behavior for his lack of friends. He therefore, carefully avoided her at school. Jean had become sensitive to name-calling, expressed violent hatred for herself, dressed like a tomboy and wanted to be a boy. She stated that if she could be an animal, she would like to be a powerful stallion and stomp people to death. Both children expressed violent outrage and hatred towards one another.

Although Mr. W. intensely disliked Erik's criticism of Jean, he permitted Erik to criticize her for what appeared to be his own fear of losing a position of power. He said, "If I correct my daughter's behavior, my son will think he's right, and it will only give him further permission to attack her." Erik was terribly confused. He was impulsive by nature, extremely anxious and never knew where he stood with his parents.

Mrs. W. constantly doubted her worth and feared abandonment by her husband. She maintained a wishful longing for the good old days and wished her husband was like he used to be, which was her way of expressing her own uncomfortable feeling of distance from her husband. Erik expressed his mother's feelings of loneliness, never having enough, disillusionment, and outrage. He was extremely aggressive, feared his aggression, and was made uncomfortable by it. He frequently expressed his wish to kill those persons who angered him. His mother once said, "He's really homicidal, isn't he?" However, more often she said, "He just uses the word 'kill' as a figure of speech."

Erik was in an unenviable position--he was assigned the role to improve his sister's behavior, which the father disliked in his wife and the mother valued and encouraged in her own daughter. At the same time he heard, "You're driving me crazy with your fighting."

The children's behavior and inner experiences were never validated. Erik was never given open permission to express his feelings. The mother failed to listen to what the children really had to say, and the father interpreted Erik's anger as disobedient and ungrateful behavior. The mother was vague in her communication style. Her irrelevant, intellectual "truths," inappropriate affect, nodding, smiling face of approval, significant silence, failure to intervene and take a stand were all interpreted as confusing messages of encouragement by the children. Often her words faintly said, "I don't like what you are doing" while her non-verbal behavior strongly and implicitly encouraged their behavior.

Erik had just encountered an experience on his way home from school when two boys attacked and kicked him; he was furious and felt humiliated. He expressed feelings of murderous retaliation in this example.

Therapist: That must have been terribly humiliating for you. (acknowledgement and permission to express his feelings)

Erik: I wasn't humiliated because they knew I had a bicycle chain with me and I would have killed them. They knew I had a weapon on me. (denial of feelings and irrelevance)

Mrs. W.: (sitting silently smiling to herself)

Therapist: When you saw them egging each other on to pick on you, what kept you around?

Mrs. W. (angrily to the therapist): The idea of turning your cheek doesn't hold anymore. Look at the Jews--if they had learned to fight back . . . (an irrelevant truth)

Erik: I'm going to kill those boys. (he was becoming more and more anxious)

Mrs. W. (smiling): It's good for him to talk about his feelings. He will get it out of his system. Anyway, anyone who behaves like that deserves to die. (As Mrs. W. failed to acknowledge Erik's murderous feelings and validate his behavior, his feelings of outrage and anxiety heightened. He had taken a

frightening stand by saying, "I'm going to kill
those boys," while the mother implicitly
encouraged this position through her manner of
communication with "Why don't you--they
deserve it."

Responsibility for behavior given to an omnipotent force by family members

Family O.: Mrs. O. called for an
appointment with the complaint that her 5-year-
old adopted son, Martin, was extremely bright
and precocious, but was showing disobedient
behavior and hyperactivity, which she hoped
could be managed with a simple course of
medication.

At the time the family was first seen,
Martin was a talkative, anxious, stubborn
child, acting as the family scapegoat to help
maintain the parents' feelings of great distance
from one another. Mrs. O. was feeling lonely
and unable to communicate with her quiet,
withdrawn, preoccupied husband. Reverend O.
was completely involved in his church activities
and spent little time at home.

Martin had been adopted in early infancy
by the Reverend and his wife after they had
been married for many years. The parents had
recently moved from another parish and missed
their family and many old friends and projected
their sadness on Martin. Martin was precocious in all his language skills; his mother
was very proud of his ability to speak two
languages, English and French. He had been
an active toddler, and had no problems in
feeding. He rocked in his crib as an infant
and was given phenobarbital for an inability to
fall asleep at night. He occasionally wet the
bed and his parents were concerned about his
poor impulse control. He was stimulus-oriented
and had to be watched constantly so that he
wouldn't dash into the street on impulse. His

pediatric neurological examination, however, was well within normal limits.

During the first interview, the mother appeared to laugh and smile whenever she became anxious or worried and had difficulty in expressing her feelings of sadness and anger. The Reverend appeared remote, preoccupied and distant and spoke in a halting, controlled voice. Mrs. O. talked for the family; she described how smart Martin was and laughed at him when he talked about his secret playmate, "the Devil, with whom he plays all the time." The "Devil" assumed and was given responsibility for Martin's behavior; Martin said, "The Devil tells me to do it." He described the Devil as a man who smells and wears a black suit (just like his father).

Mrs. O. told Martin of his adoption in the following way: "God brought you to us, Martin. He tells us when to feed you, when to spank you, when you are bad, when to dress you, when to give you things, and when to be angry." It soon became apparent that God was having a dialogue with the Devil. The family rule was that no one assumed direct responsibility for his own behavior. God assumed responsibility for the Reverend and Mrs. O.; the Devil was responsible for whatever Martin did. As Martin talked about the Devil his mother responded with a "double-level message." She simultaneously disapproved with words and approved with nonverbal laughter and smiling, which sustained and stimulated Martin's interest in the Devil. When he was told by the therapist that there is no Devil, he said emphatically, "Well, I'm the Devil."

At a later visit, when Martin came alone with his father, he said in the waiting room, "I won't do anything," at which point he wanted to be forced and the Reverend appeared exasperated and helpless. Martin put his hands over his ears and said, "I'm not going to listen. No, I'm not going to do anything. I'm going to be stupid." He then rudely told his father to "shut-up" and his father became extremely angry. The "Devil" was in control and the Reverend's only recourse was to frighten him with what God would do to him for his bad behavior. Martin replied, "I'm not bad--it's the Devil telling me to do it." Martin talked about how he would like to kill everyone and how happy he would feel when he could do just that. He would kill his mother and his daddy and all the good people except for his friend, the Devil. "You can't get rid of the Devil because he is magic--he chokes people with lots of hands." (He drew pictures of Devils with lots of hands.) With a smile on his face, Martin said, "He's so happy, he kills everybody." As the father listened to this he became more and more distraught and immobile. When the Reverend and his son returned home he told his wife who, in turn, attacked Martin with, "Why did you tell the doctor that you wanted to kill us?" Mrs. O. encouraged Martin's constant companion, the imaginary play friend, the Devil, by her continued combined amusement and anger. She also had feelings of desperate rage and resentment towards this child whom she frequently beat.

The Reverend said, "I don't spend enough time with Martin," and later he said, "He wastes my time and I'd rather be doing something else." At one time Martin said, "I can't get father to notice me."

In an experience with role playing, Martin sat behind the desk and played doctor. The therapist became the mother of a recalcitrant little girl played by the mother.

Therapist: Doctor, how would you manage the

problem I have in getting my little girl to go
to bed at night?

<u>Dr. Martin</u> (seriously): You beat her with a
stick.

<u>Reverend</u> (turning to the mother accusingly):
You're always saying to him "If you don't do
what I say, I'll beat you until I break your
bones."

During the role playing Martin showed a need to have
limits set for himself and to have things taken away from
him. He felt his mother shouldn't punish, that the punishment should come from the child and the child should
punish himself. Martin was fascinated by the good side
of himself.

Martin was clearly more than Mrs. O. could handle
by herself. She needed help from her husband who
remained remote and ineffectual. The Reverend had
developed an ulcer, chewed antacid tablets, and took to
preparing next Sunday's sermon. Mrs. O. indirectly
expressed her resentment toward her husband through her
son. Her inappropriate amusement encouraged Martin's
abusiveness and unmanageable behavior toward his father;
in turn, the father appeared preoccupied and ineffectual.
God and the Devil were made responsible for behavior so
that no one was held accountable for himself and, consequently, all manner of inappropriate behavior became per-
missible.

Although the parents felt victimized by Martin, they
dropped from therapy once attention gradually shifted from
Martin to their own problems of distance and communication. They had wanted a prescription to control Martin's
behavior but were not ready to change the family system.
The mother who had to work in the morning complained
about the high living costs and medical expenses. When
the father discontinued therapy over the telephone, he
said, "I don't have the time to come for this kind of
business--I think he'll outgrow it--he's going to have
this problem for a long time and we can't afford it--he's
just spoiled--what he needs is more friends." These

excuses were presented to avoid a focus on the way the parents' own conflicts were being expressed through Martin's behavior.

5 Approach Used in the Treatment and Management
   of Childhood Learning and Behavior Problems

In the treatment and management of childhood learning
and behavior problems early assessment of the child's
neurodevelopmental state and function of the family system
will often help prevent or lessen the catastrophic events
that lead to social maladjustment and disrupted family
development. The comprehensive management of all childhood learning and behavior problems should include: (a)
early detection of high-risk children, (b) a meaningful
assessment of child development and family function, (c)
special academic help with the development of specific
skills, i.e., special class placement, disability group
placement, one-to-one tutoring at home or at school, (d)
a trial on medication for the management of any associated
hyperactivity, distractibility, short attention span, poor
impulse control, and/or poor tolerance for frustration, and
(e) ongoing family therapy when indicated to assist the
child and family in interaction together, particularly as it
relates to the youngster's learning problems. The therapist
must learn to work at different interphases--between the
child and parents, between the family and the school, and
finally between the family and the community.

Early Detection of High-Risk Children

Early detection of specific learning disorders prevents
the disturbing events that effect the child and his family
when the problems are allowed to go unrecognized.
DeHirsch, Jansky, and Langford (1966) followed pre-school
children over a 20-year period and found significant
correlation between certain motor and cognitive skills and
failure to read or a delay in the onset of reading. Their
findings of particular predictive diagnostic value for the
kindergarten child were: (a) delayed onset and poor

quality of expressive language ability, (b) poor spontaneous expressive language ability with sparse vocabulary and poor organization in telling a story, and (c) difficulty in holding a pencil and copying written symbols.

Assessment of Child Development and Family Function

The neurodevelopmental-family assessment functions as the first stage of therapy. It has become the key to the total therapeutic process which begins with the first family-consultant encounter. The therapeutic process is not a separate function which begins at the close of the evaluation, for assessment, improved awareness, and change leading to growth are interdependent processes in dynamic reciprocal relationship with one another. (See Figure 1.)

FIGURE 1

THERAPEUTIC PROCESS

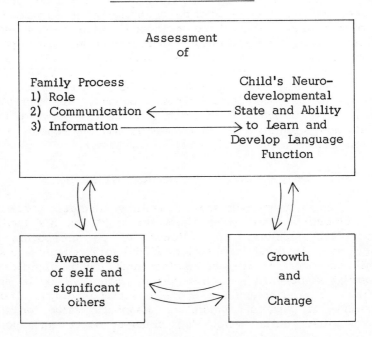

The formal assessment includes a 1-1/2-hour conjoint family interview conducted by the pediatrician, psychiatrist, or psychiatric social worker trained in Gestalt-
oriented conjoint family therapy techniques and child
development. This one person acts as coordinator-
therapist. The family interview is followed by the
psychologist's developmental assessment, a pediatric
neurological examination, speech and language evaluation,
and an educational evaluation. The assessment is concluded by the coordinator-therapist in a session held for
summary and planning.

The process assessment of the child and family provides information about "what is going on" between the
parents and child and how it relates to "where" the child
is in his learning and language development. The descriptive information determines "what needs to be done" to
bring about change for more effective learning and improved
family interaction. The process assessment of the child is
concerned with the child's ability to learn and acquire
written and spoken language function (speech, writing,
spelling, arithmetic), style of learning, activity level,
ability to handle frustration and anger, attentiveness,
social awareness, and ability to problem-solve and
approach a task.

Haley (1967) outlined three theories which can be
used as the basis for the process assessment of the
family. He sees the family as a system determined by (a)
parental role assignment (Bell & Vogel, 1968b) with
equilibrium maintained by resolution of role conflict
(Speigel, 1957), (b) the process of interactional patterns
of communication, and (c) the informational system, i.e.,
the given task of the family and the expected output.
With these theories in mind it is possible to obtain
descriptive information about the family's patterns of communication, expectations, goals, values, rules, roles,
myths, manner of expressing feelings, handling differences,
and the way responsibility for self and other is assumed
within the family system.

Initial Conjoint Family Interview

The assessment of child development and family

process begins during the initial conjoint family interview.
At this time, the developmental history of the child and
the family chronology are developed.   Whenever possible,
a review of information obtained from the school and
family physician is made prior to the evaluation to gain
a   better   understanding   of   the   child's   and   family's
problems.   Before discussing the reasons for referral, time
is spent in getting acquainted to help place the family and
therapist at ease.   Throughout, there is an emphasis on
process rather than content.   This automatically avoids
value judgments, the use of blame, labels, and complicated diagnostic terminology.   An accepting, understanding
manner is maintained throughout, keeping in mind the
family's   good   intentions   and   human   condition.   The
techniques of restatement, clarification, and carefully-
timed process interpretations can assist the family members
in gaining a better understanding of how they feel and
what they are doing.   The child and parents are helped to
openly   express   their   feelings   of   worrisome   diagnostic
labels, fears, and feelings of self-blame or blame heaped
upon them by neighbors, schools, or other professionals.

Interviewing techniques.   The following questions*
may be used to initiate the interview, obtain the developmental history, and develop the family chronology.   All of
these questions need not and usually cannot be answered
during one interview.   Most of these questions focus on
process, not content, with particular attention given to
"what" and "how" it is being said rather than to the
words themselves.   Attention is given to non-verbal facial
expressions, tone of voice, and body movements.   Who
acts as the family spokesman? How does the family
communicate?   handle feelings?   accept differences of
opinion?

"What are your major concerns as parents?
What questions or what would you like to learn
        or have answered by this study?
When did you first become concerned?

_____

*most of which were developed by Mrs. Wilma Buckman,
Psychiatric Social Worker in the Child Study Unit, and
extended by the author

What have you learned from other professionals?
What do you see as your child's problems?
How is your child affected by these problems?
What did you tell your youngster about why you were bringing him here?
How do you know when your child is upset or worried?
How do you find out?
How does it affect you?
How do each of you show your anger?
How do you react toward anger?
How does he let you know how he is feeling?"

Questions directed to the child have to do with what he likes to do in school and how he views his family and himself.

"What gives you trouble?
What have you been told about coming to the interview?
What do the children tease you about?
How do you tell when your mother and father are angry?
How do your brothers and sisters tease you?
How do you bother your brothers and sisters?
How do you know how to bother your mother and father?
What do you do that makes your parents angry?
If you had three wishes, what would you wish for?
Children have lively imaginations--what do you imagine?
If you could change things at home, what would you change?
What would you like to ask from each of your parents?
If you could change something about your parents, what would you change?
What could your parents do differently that would make life happier for you around the house?"

Questions that the therapist can ask himself after

observation of the child in play are:

> "How does the child relate to the examiner?
> How does he approach a new situation?
> What is his reaction to the play material?
> Does he show normal curiosity for his age?
> Does he use toys in an age-appropriate manner?
> Does he use toys in a sex-appropriate manner?
> Does he need support or reassurance to continue playing?
> Does he develop themes in his play and interrelate use of toys?
> How does he persist at various tasks?
> What is the theme of the play?
> Can he accept help, suggestions, or directions?
> Is he comprehending conversation appropriate for his age?
> How does he respond to winning? to losing?
> Describe the child's motor activity.
> Describe the child's affect or characteristic mood.
> How does this child cope with anxiety?
> Is this child creative?"

A reliable developmental history can be obtained by using specific growth landmarks as points of reference; questions that require a "yes" or "no" answer or value judgments have very limited value. A parent might say "yes" to "Did he have good language development?" when, in fact, the child might not be speaking as yet. Useful information about the child's language development can be obtained from "what," "when," and "how" questions about onset, quality, and quantity of babbling, use of isolated words, phrases, sentences, ability to follow directions, ability to use meaningful words in speech, etc.

The pregnancy history is important as it relates to how the mother felt, medication used, how both parents accepted the idea of pregnancy, their reactions during it and at the time of delivery. It is important to learn about the nature of the labor and the condition of the baby at the time of delivery.

"How did he take his feedings, sleep, and
    respond to cuddling as an infant?
When and how did he begin to sit and walk,
    tie shoes, ride a tricycle? a bicycle?
When did he begin to say the letters of the
    alphabet in order, copy the letters down
    in dictation?
How did the child handle separation from his
    mother on entering school, get along with
    other children in the family, handle frus-
    tration, show anger, express feelings,
    use language to express himself?
What ability did he show in telling a story on
    entering kindergarten?"

It is important to respond to the parents' feelings at
the moment as well as to deal with their feelings about
the past.   The child and parents can understand how they
have come to be through the development of a cast of
characters in the family chronology (Satir, 1964).   This
provides information about the models for child and
parental behavior and permits the important idea of individual differences to be developed.   Questions useful in
obtaining the family chronology are:

"In recalling your own childhood, how were you
    raised?
How did your parents think a child should be
    managed--strict or lenient?
Can you recall what you might have said as a
    child about how you would raise your own
    children?
What was it like when you were growing up?
Who made up your family?
How did school go for you?
How far did your parents go in school?
What did you argue about with your parents?
How does the management of your children
    differ from that of your own parents?
How did the two of you come to meet (husband
    and wife)?
What are the things that attracted you to each
    other?

What pleasure or fun do you have together?
with your child? (The same question is
asked of the child about what fun he has
with his mother and father.)
What differences of opinion do you have in the
management of your children?"

The importance of difference may also be brought out
by asking the parents how they are alike and different,
how their own parents handled their differences, and how
they handle their own differences. Ideally, the parents
should be able to say to one another and to their children,
"I will still like you or love you even though you have a
difference of opinion."

Pediatric Neurological Examination

The pediatric neurological examination will help to
measure maturity by observation of the child's activity
level, control of posture, quality of gait, balance, the
child's conception of his own body image, body parts,
position in space, establishment of laterality, and extent
and degree of cortical inhibition. The tests of neurological
function for the school age child are presented in
Appendix I.

Developmental Assessment

The psychologist's developmental assessment will
provide information about the child's learning strengths and
weaknesses and his ability to adapt socially. His
behavior is observed throughout the test situation for
activity level, span of attention, rapport, response to
failure, manner of problem solving, degree of confidence,
and attitude toward the examiner. The psychologist often
supplements the educational consultant's evaluation with
tests of achievement in oral word recognition, spelling of
dictated words, and written solution of arithmetic
problems.

General intelligence is measured either by the
Stanford-Binet Intelligence Scale or the Wechsler Intelligence Scale for Children (WISC). Generally, the WISC is
selected for the school age child, who obviously has

expressive language and performance skills, since this test requires verbal answers as well as performance tasks.

Tests of visual-motor integrative function include the Bender Visual-Motor Gestalt Test, the Beery Developmental Form Sequence Test, the Frostig Developmental Test of Visual Perception, and finally the Draw-A-Person Test. Specific tests for visual memory are given with the Detroit Test of Learning Aptitude, the Benton Visual Retention Test, the Graham and Kendall Memory for Designs Test, and the visual sequential memory test on the Illinois Test of Psycholinguistic Abilities (ITPA). For auditory memory, the Spencer Sentence Memory Test, the Detroit Test of Learning Aptitude, and the auditory sequential memory test on the Illinois Test of Psycholinguistic Abilities are used. Auditory discrimination is evaluated by the Wepman Auditory Discrimination Test. Tests of receptive language include the Peabody Picture Vocabulary Test where the child points to a picture to match a word said by the examiner, the Quick Test of Receptive Vocabulary, where the child points to named objects, or the auditory and visual reception tests of the Illinois Test of Psycholinguistic Abilities. A list of all tests may be found in Appendix II.

Educational Evaluation

The education consultant provides information about where the child's development is in the continuum of reading, writing, spelling, and arithmetic. The Durrell Analysis of Reading Difficulty, the Monroe Reading Aptitude Test, the Gates-McKillop Reading Diagnostic Test, the Gray Oral Reading Test, and the Gilmore Oral Reading Test evaluate the mechanics and comprehension of silent and oral reading. The child's phonic, auditory, visual, and visual-motor skills are reviewed by task analysis, i.e., what does the task require and what is the child actually able to do? A list of these tests is compiled in Appendix III.

Summary and Planning Session

Once the conjoint family interview, pediatric neurological examination, developmental assessment, educational evaluation, and speech and language evaluation have

been completed, the findings are coordinated and interpreted to the family in a session held for summary and
planning. This is usually conducted with the parents and
child together, depending upon the findings and the age of
the child; the circumstances vary from one family to
another. There are some findings that everyone in the
family should share, especially if this new information
can clarify some misunderstandings that are held by the
entire family. For example, when a child is not "dumb"
or "bad," an explanation is necessary to describe the
child's difficulty in sitting still, problems in expressing
himself with words, and that he might use crying or
striking out as a way to express anger and frustration.
Uncomfortable parental feelings of guilt, blame, helplessness, and resentment can be lessened by offering an
understanding of the difficulties they must be experiencing.
It is therefore helpful to assume that the parents have
tried their best, that such problems are understandably
confusing, and that the situation is difficult for everyone.
Throughout the discussion, the child's and parents'
strengths should be emphasized; this also helps diminish
the parents' tension and fears based on real or unfounded
information. Specific terms must be defined, for each term
has a specific meaning for each person.

If the child has significant overall problems in
learning, the term "retarded" may mean to a parent that
the child will stop learning and eventually need to be
institutionalized. This is generally not the case, unless
one is dealing with the untrainable retarded. The parents
need the assurance that the child will continue to learn,
though perhaps at a slower rate. Although he probably
will not be able to catch up with other children of his own
age, he will progress and be able to achieve some degree
of independence through appropriate training.

If, on the other hand, the child has normal intelligence with specific deficits in specific processes of
learning, this can be explained by describing the specific
processes that have interfered with the development of the
acquired language skills (spelling, arithmetic, handwriting,
reading). This is accomplished by explaining the task
faced by the child and how these specific problems relate
to his present and future school experience.

The following questions are helpful in giving the parents an opportunity to express their fears, particularly as they relate to the child's problems:

"What would you like to be able to hear?
What could you imagine would be the worst thing you could learn from our findings during the evaluation?"

Pressing worries and concerns answered in response to the above questions usually are:

"I would hate to hear that he has problems about which nothing could be done.
I worry he'll drop out of school and get caught up in the drug scene.
I worry he'll stop learning.
I'd hate to find out that he is emotionally disturbed (for I would conclude that I am to blame).
I could not tolerate having a brain-damaged child (for this means that nothing can be done and it may be due to the time he fell from his crib when I wasn't looking).
I worry that he may turn out just like his schizophrenic, mentally retarded, emotionally disturbed aunt or alcoholic Uncle Bob (a bad seed).

The therapist can use this opportunity to clarify confusing diagnostic labels by avoiding complicated terminology and focusing on descriptive information about what the child and family are doing.

A positive change often occurs in the family's outlook by the time recommendations are made for future management in regard to ongoing family therapy, medication, or attention to the child's special academic needs. Many of the early defenses will be down. This change will have come from an improved understanding of the problems and the parents have had an opportunity to express their feelings openly. When the family is functional and the problems are identifiable and manageable, the assessment and appropriate follow-up may be all the

child and family need.   However, when ongoing family
therapy is indicated, this improved outlook may be
transient and deceive the family into thinking that nothing
more needs to be done.   This phenomena must be recog-
nized in order to help the parents continue in treatment.

The recommendation for continued family therapy is
generally facilitated by the family's favorable experience
with this new approach and the feeling of hope directs the
need for continuing in therapy.   When making these recommendations, man's strong resistance to change based on
fear of the unknown and loss of control must be understood.   There are fears about being "found out," being
different, unique or crazy, or there are inner conflicts of
greed and lust, good and bad, concealment and exposure,
aggression and passivity, difference and likeness, masculinity and femininity, which tend to keep a tenacious hold
on the status quo.   Often, the parents may refuse therapy
if they need to hold onto an inoperative myth, or they may
accept therapy with the hope that the therapist will help to
continue the myth.

The decision for recommending family therapy is
based on whether or not the family is considered functional.   A family may be considered functional when there
are open patterns of communication, where there is freedom
to express feelings openly, each person is taught to
assume responsibility for himself, and individual differences
are given a positive value.   Constant change and flux is
required to maintain a state of equilibrium.   Changes occur
in individual family members as a never-ending process of
self-assessment, improved self-awareness, and the need
for change.   Part of the therapeutic process is concerned
in helping those individuals in a dysfunctional family who
are unable to accomplish these tasks alone.   Therapeutic
intervention is therefore necessary when the child is used
as a scapegoat, when assumed or assigned roles and
survival myths are no longer operational, where patterns
of communication are fixed and closed, individual differences are interpreted as a form of rejection, and/or individual family members are unable to assume responsibility
for themselves.

A discussion of Gestalt-oriented conjoint family

therapy is presented in Chapter 6.

Educational Therapy

In the past it was thought that once a child's disability in processes of learning had been defined, management should be directed toward this disability. The child was "taught to the disability" with remediation of any language skill directed toward overcoming and improving the particular disability. This approach has gradually given way to the idea of teaching to the strength, i.e., toward the functional pathway for learning. From experience, teachers have learned that the child will stop learning and resist any attempt to help him when unrelenting efforts of remediation are directed only toward his weaknesses. This does not mean that the child should not receive help in the areas where function is most disabled; however, successful learning through alternative pathways seems more profitable and permits the child to feel success rather than failure. The educational needs vary for each child and the educational programs and approaches seem to vary with the individual and with the school. Individual attention is necessary and, depending on the circumstances, there is a need for one-to-one tutoring, part-time disability group placement, or small, full-time classes for the educationally handicapped.

Drug Therapy

The use of psychotropic drugs in the management of children with hyperkinetic behavior has become a useful adjunct. Unfortunately, there has been an abuse of these drugs by parents and doctors who search for magic cures. Drugs are often started without proper evaluation, without educational and family therapy, and, because of the complex nature of these children, without criteria for the diagnosis and indications for their use. The variability of symptoms in different settings and the difficulties in setting double-blind studies partially account for the variance in opinions on the effectiveness of different drugs. The attitude of the family towards drugs, as well as unrecognized psychogenic factors, can also often interfere with the effectiveness of drugs in some children.

Antidepressant drugs are most commonly used for hyperactivity, distractibility, short attention span, impulsivity, and poor tolerance for frustration, and include the minor psychomotor stimulants and major psychic energizers. Dextroamphetamine (Dexedrine^R), widely used for hyperkinetic behavior since 1937, acts as a mild antidepressant, depresses the appetite and, when effective, decreases the activity level. The dose for children ranges from 2.5 to 10 mg. bid. Ritalin^R, another antidepressant used for the treatment of hyperkinetic behavior in children, is considered to be much less habituating than the amphetamines and decreases the activity level by cutting down on the distractibility and inattentiveness. Ritalin^R is a psychic stimulant and antileptic which acts on the reticular activating system. The usual dose of Ritalin^R is 10 to 20 mg. bid given in the morning and at noon (not generally recommended after 3 o'clock in the afternoon). Imipramine (Tofranil^R), 50 to 100 mg. per day, has recently been reported to be one of the more efficacious pharmacotherapeutic agents (Greenberg, 1971). Other drugs have also been recommended for treatment of "minimal brain dysfunction" syndromes and for children with hyperactivity and learning disabilities (Fowler & Millichap, 1967). However, no drug should be used without firm indication, careful control, and due precaution for toxicity (Eisenberg, 1968, 1959). Drugs are neither panaceas nor poisonous, however, no drug should be used longer than necessary and its dosage should be reduced periodically, with the goal of cessation if symptoms do not return on a lower dosage (Millichap, 1968).

6   Gestalt-oriented Conjoint Family Therapy

The principles of Perls' Gestalt Therapy and Satir's Conjoint Family Therapy have been uniquely combined by Dr. Alan Leveton* and Mrs. Wilma Buckman[+] of the Child Study Unit to form the basis for the approach used in the assessment and ongoing treatment of families in the management of childhood learning and behavior problems.

The discussion that follows is an introduction to the ideas held in each discipline and to the way each discipline enhances the other when used together. Therefore, the reader is referred to the texts of Frederick Perls' Gestalt Therapy Verbatim (1969) and Virginia Satir's Conjoint Family Therapy (1964) as the place to begin.

The place for family therapy in the management of these problems seems obvious when one begins to consider the family as a system, with each member serving a functional role to maintain a dynamic state of equilibrium. When this state is disrupted by any one member, change follows within the system itself.

From our work with families, a dysfunctional family allows little opportunity for change in the child's behavior if the system remains unchanged. We see children with obscure learning problems disrupt the family system by threatening the family's value system and the parents' self-esteem. The situation may be further complicated

*Psychiatrist, Child Study Unit, Department of Pediatrics, University of California San Francisco Medical Center
[+]Psychiatric Social Worker, Child Study Unit, Department of Pediatrics, University of California San Francisco Medical Center

71

when the child becomes the scapegoat and eventually the Identified Patient if his problems direct attention from serious conflicts with or between the parents. On the other hand, children experience stress from inappropriate role assignments and closed patterns of communication when a family becomes dysfunctional as a result of unresolved parental conflicts and poor parental models.

A Gestalt-oriented conjoint family therapy approach has proved to be an extremely effective and, therefore, exciting experience for achieving success in the management of children's learning and behavior problems. The excitement comes when significant change is made possible through an understanding of the dynamic process of family interaction. By working directly with the family, the therapist has the opportunity to act as an agent of change by assuming an active role in bringing about improved communication within the family, particularly when the communication patterns place the child in a double-bind (see page 40). A very important advantage this method has over individual psychotherapy for the child is the inherent provision for helping the parents. When a child needs help, so do the parents. Individual psychotherapy with the child does provide an often-needed ally in the therapist, however, the parents are further isolated with feelings of blame and the poor communication within the family either worsens or continues unchanged.

The discussion of therapeutic approaches is extremely difficult since so much controversy exists among the children's helping professionals concerning the efficacy of one psychotherapeutic method over another. Therefore, the task of describing and perhaps even feeling the need to defend the use of Gestalt and conjoint family therapy becomes formidable. The difficulty is further heightened by knowing that the ideas and process can probably be conveyed effectively only through direct observation and demonstration. In spite of these obstacles, one may persist in believing that it is possible to persuade the reader toward understanding without emotional and pejorative defenses.

Following some general remarks, a discussion of the basic concepts of these two disciplines will be made as they are used in interviewing and therapy during the neuro-developmental-family assessment and ongoing family therapy.   A case will be discussed at the end to describe the therapist's task in helping a child and family by using these methods and to show the particular way the various problems revealed themselves.

In working with children, whatever techniques might happen to be used at the moment, it is useful to hold three concepts in mind as a basis for what needs to be done.   They are: (a) the important effect the child's unique ability to learn and develop language function has on the child's and family's behavior, (b) the child is a growing organism with an everchanging substrate, and (c) the child is an integral part of a family system that functions as a unit.   It is important to remember that techniques are worthless when they become an end in themselves or when the person using them knows not why or where he is going with them.

The family system functions or dysfunctions, as the case may be, depending on the way the parents play their role of leadership with respect to the child and the way they establish models of behavior through their own values and style of communication.

With these ideas in mind, it is certainly not necessary to always have every member of the family together on each visit.   As a matter of fact, one can generally work more successfully with only two or three members at a time; however, it is possible to "bring to life" and into the room an important family member distanced by geographical location or someone who has long since passed.

Usually, after the initial assessment has been conducted, the focus gradually begins to shift away from the child and Identified Patient.   This occurs after the child has been made more comfortable by new family insights and more reasonable expectations from his family and school.   During the assessment one can begin to get an idea of how the family system works, what the patterns of communication are like, who is assuming what role, and of those experiencing difficulty, who is in the best position to accept help. In the form of a hunch or hypothesis, any information gained like this can be discussed with the family from time to time.

A real advantage of seeing the family together is being able to avoid hearing a single viewpoint of how the husband, wife, or child seems to experience someone or something. A great deal of the patient's and therapist's time is wasted when one sees or listens to one person apart from the family. As a therapist, I want to see and hear for myself what seems to be going on and to be there to help the family members "see it like it is" and express their feelings openly. I need to comment on the way it appears to me and be able to help them comment on what they might be experiencing at the moment. Work can be done with only the parents together or with a child and his parents together. If, for example, the child is with the parents, the child can either actively participate by speaking for himself or can play or draw while listening to what is going on. Naturally, the child will be excused at any time, determined by anyone, depending on the content of the discussion. When the child is present, it is help-ful to understand how the parents set limits and how they feel about certain observed behavior during the hour.

Role playing can be used extensively in one form or another. Sometimes the therapist might play the child with the mother or allow the child to be the parent with the therapist as the child. There are endless possibilities depending on the problem. The family members may play the roles of each other or "be" their own mothers or fathers and in this way learn more about themselves and others by actually living through an experience. When a patient appears to be resentful or actively avoiding a difficult position, that person can be helped to play both sides of himself to find out what position or issue "fits" or in other words where he is stuck in resolving a conflict within himself, i.e., conflicts of lust, control, passivity, etc. These conflicts account for avoidance and resistance that stands in the way of completing the gestalt or unfinished business. An oversimplified example would be to ask the weak-passive side of a person to tell the strong-aggressive side what he resents and vice versa. Talking back and forth with oneself either ends in an impasse or in a resolution of conflict. The impasse results when a person is unable to change by giving up something and therefore remains exactly where he is.

Sometimes the child needs to be seen alone for a few visits. For example, Cindy, a 9-year-old girl, was afraid to walk alone to her own room down a short, well-lit corridor. She feared "people" would jump out at her from behind the doors or throw out a trap to catch her as she walked. She was also afraid someone might jump out of the toilet bowl. She handled these fears by taking a parent or her 2-1/2-old sister with her. If they weren't available she could prevent catastrophy by whistling.

Her mother was a fearful woman who was afraid of the outside world. She had experienced a total absence of feeling for Cindy at the time of her birth and she had marked feelings of discomfort for not having a "normal" response.

In brief, I had Cindy alternate between being the boogy man and the Cindy who would like to rid herself of him. During this time Cindy showed great interest and excitement in playing both roles and finally got up the courage to hit and kick this evil person out of her life. After only two or three sessions Cindy began to be less fearful and therefore feel more comfortable. At the same time it was also necessary to work with the mother's feelings of guilt and insecurity. It became apparent to the mother how her own fears reinforced Cindy's and how they identified with one another. As long as the mother needed to walk with Cindy to her room the idea that there could be a boogy man remained.

Direct play or observed play with the child under the age of nine or ten can often help the child deal with real issues of control and mastery. Discussion about drawings, construction or verbalized fantasy can also be useful in helping the child and family understand what the child is dramatizing, for example, superman, victim, rescuer, good or bad guy.

Once the Identified Patient is feeling more comfortable, the parents may seek help for another child or themselves. The Identified Patient may feel a sense of relief to know that he is not "all bad" or the "whole problem" and gains respect for his parents who are able to ask for help when in trouble.

In whatever way the members of the family are seen, whether alone or as a family together, it is important to keep the task of therapy in the context of the real and not imagined family.

Not all children with learning and language disorders live in a dysfunctional family. However, many of these children are the primary cause of family dysfunction or become the Identified Patient in an already dysfunctional family. For some families, the only psychotherapeutic intervention necessary is the assessment itself which helps to define the problems, outlining through new insights appropriate expectations from the family, special academic needs, and the possible need for medication. Many families, however, are found at the time of the assessment to be dysfunctional, indicating the need for ongoing family therapy.

Basic Concepts of Conjoint Family Therapy and Gestalt Therapy

While Satir's Conjoint Family Therapy methods direct attention to the family's system as a whole, Perls' Gestalt Therapy is concerned with the whole individual made up of many parts. Whereas Conjoint Family Therapy provides a useful method for understanding and working with the family with a focus upon change which comes from improved interactional patterns of communication within the family system, Gestalt therapy is primarily directed toward the individual with change that comes through improved self-awareness and the resolution of intrapsychic conflicts. Both approaches are concerned with the therapist's active role in bringing about change through improved awareness of self and by dealing with the here and now (Perls, 1969).

Gestalt therapy gets in touch with the obvious through a continuum of awareness established by the therapist's feedback of what is seen and heard. It was

Perls' belief that the most important unfinished situations will always emerge and therefore can be handled. The person functions badly when thousands of unfinished situations demand completion. The task of the therapist is to help the individual find out where he is "stuck" by determining what the individual wants to avoid. In this way the individual is actually helped to know and experience himself better and function as a whole. He also felt that verbal communication is usually a lie, that the real communication is beyond words, i.e., in voice, posture, and gestures.

Satir has described the Identified Patient, who is often the child, as the one most obviously effected by a pained marital relationship and the one most subjected to dysfunctional parenting. She has not, however, discussed in her text the reasons why a particular child is selected as the Identified Patient, nor emphasized the effect childhood learning disorders have on parental function. Dr. Helen Gofman (Allmond & Gofman, 1971) has been one of the first to become interested in the effect these problems have on family function which has added an important dimension to Satir's ideas concerning the etiology of family dysfunction.

Perls' techniques focus on the individual with an emphasis on the here and now and telling it like it is with full acknowledgment that each moment in the present is dependent upon what has happened in the past. Each family member has the opportunity to check out how each individual experiences himself and how he is being experienced by others. (Laing, 1967, believes that we never experience that which is being experienced by another--as therapists, we can only hope to assist in an improved awareness of that which is being experienced.)

Since both Gestalt and Conjoint Family Therapy, when used alone or combined, focus on process rather than content, the use of blame and value judgments is automatically avoided. In both, the therapist is not a passive sounding board sitting in judgment as a sympathetic ally. He assumes an active role to acknowledge feelings openly and emphasizes the positive value of individual difference.

The therapist actively comments on verbal and non-verbal communication to direct the way for open patterns of communication. One way this is done is by restatement and clarification of "what" was really said with words and "what" the words and non-verbal communication really say as the underlying process of communication.

The following example of a process interpretation is taken from a family therapy session where close attention was given to the significant and powerful non-verbal communication expressed in body posture, tone of voice, and facial expressions. These observations were "fed back" to the patient.

Wife (directed to her husband in an angry, sad voice): I'd never call you by the name of my first husband. (The husband occasionally made mistakes and called his present wife by his first wife's name.)

Husband (silent with a distant look and half-smile)

Therapist: Your voice sounds angry to me and I see tears in your eyes. (Pause) You sound disappointed and betrayed.

Wife (cries)

Therapist: I hear you say, "If you really love me, you wouldn't be so thoughtless."

Wife (directed to her husband, stamping her feet, with a flushed face): I don't feel loved. I don't have to stay with anyone who doesn't love me.

This interaction shows the way the therapist can deal with underlying feelings rather than the content which, in this case, would be what name each calls the other.

The therapist comments on what he "sees" and "hears" and helps each family member to comment on how they experience each other. One way to accomplish this is to have the family members speak directly to one another, rather than through the therapist. The encouragement of "I" and "you" statements improves communication by avoiding the editorial "we," "one," and "you" which helps the individual to enjoy the pleasure of standing behind his or her own words. The use of first person allows individuals to become closer to their feelings rather than remaining at a distance through the use of vague forms.

Communication is also improved by the therapist's comments on discrepancies, either in content or between what is said and how the person appears. The therapist can say, "I'm confused; I'm hearing two different things" or "I see you're laughing, yet you have tears in your eyes." "When you just spoke to your son, your words said 'Don't burn down the house, Honey,' yet you had a smile on your face and laughter in your voice."

Case Discussion

A child and his family will be followed through their course in therapy in response to a neurodevelopmental-family approach in which Gestalt and Conjoint Family Therapy methods were used.

This family, as others who remain in therapy, determined their own movement and progress. Their discomfort, awareness of problems, and their own willingness to work made change possible. Their problems appeared sequestrated and were always more serious than the family had intended them to appear. This accounted in part for an observed pattern where each stormy period was preceded by a period of quiescence and talk of discontinuing therapy.

(T = Therapist, L = Larry, the Identified Patient, M = Mark, the stepbrother, Mrs. R. = the mother, and Mr. R. = the father.)

Family R.: Larry, the Identified Patient, was an 8-year-old boy who was referred to the University by his school and pediatrician for problems with hyperactivity, rage, impulsivity, and delayed reading skills. He came in with his recently married father, stepmother, and her 11-year-old son. His parents appeared compatable and mutually supportive and his stepmother seemed to be the one most concerned about his problems. Although it was learned much later that the parents had problems with and between themselves, they were not made apparent or disclosed at this time.

Mrs. R., a cultural anthropologist, presented herself to the therapist and to her husband as a competent, well-adjusted, self-assured woman whose life and marriage would be perfect were it not for her stepson's difficult behavior and her husband's poor handling of these difficulties. She appeared cheerful, competent, and unusually insightful in what appeared to be a "one-up" relationship with her husband for Mr. R. had less formal education and lacked her confident and knowledgeable approach to child rearing. Mr. R. seemed proud of his wife and wanted to rely upon her as a tower of strength.

Mr. R., for the most part, seemed remote. He spoke with difficulty in a slow, distant manner and had trouble talking about his feelings. He was content to have his wife speak for the family. Although Mark, Larry's new stepbrother, was included in the first visits, he was not actually brought into therapy until four or five months later after Mrs. R. had developed a feeling of trust in the therapist and Mark's acting-out behavior and her difficult relationship with him could no longer remain hidden.

Since early infancy Larry had had a history of gastrointestinal allergy and hay fever. He was maintained on a highly restrictive, hypoallergenic diet which had taken on life-threatening, survival significance for his father. His father and referring doctor described him as a disorganized, hyperactive, unmanageable toddler. At age five he was placed in the physical custody of his father, twelve months after his parents' divorce when his natural mother and kindergarten teacher were unable to manage his difficult behavior. As a consequence, Mr. R. retired from his successful electrical contracting business to stay home and act as mother. He felt sorry for Larry and saw him as a "sick" and "motherless" child. Mr. R. became solicitous and over-protective. Larry took advantage of his father's vulnerability by playing on his sympathy. He insisted on being fed, dressed, and driven to and from school. He dawdled over dressing and cried that his walk to school was too far. Larry's dependency seemed to be based in part on his father's lack of trust in him and his father's wish to stay in control. After four months of therapy Mrs. R. complained, "My husband is still wiping Larry's nose." Mrs. R.'s voice was adamant and critical, while Mr. R. became more quiet and non-verbal. Generally, Mr. R. talked without much spontaneity in a slow, groaning voice.

Mrs. R. felt Larry was "blackmailing" her. She said, "I resent him because he takes too much from me, from my son, and from my relationship with my husband." She also experienced a feeling of being torn by the demands the children made. At one point, the therapist asked the children to hold their mother by the hand and pull at the same time. Mark was unable to assert himself and held back while Larry almost pulled his stepmother to the floor. Mark's tendency to hold back prevented him from having a closer relationship with his new stepfather. In general, he was unable to take the initiative and make room for himself with others. Mark was jealous and resentful of the attention Larry received from his dependency and temper tantrums. At times the parents efforts to satisfy Larry appeared like the hopeless task of filling a bottomless pit.

Almost from the beginning Larry's hyperactive behavior was significantly reduced by a trial on Ritalin 10 mg. bid so that he became somewhat easier to handle. His hyperactivity was felt to be due in part to his neurodevelopmental state and his experienced loss of his natural mother (Malmquist, 1971). Following the developmental assessment his parents and school gained a better understanding of his specific learning problems and Larry's outlook improved when he began to receive appropriate help at school. As these changes occurred the focus of therapy began to shift to the problems of his stepmother and her 11-year-old son. As stated before, Mrs. R. felt and gave the impression that the problems she was having with her son, if any, were the results of Larry's pesty intrusions on Mark's privacy at home.

For a while both boys came in with their parents and then only Mark and his parents were seen. It became apparent that Mrs. R. and Mark had had a difficult relationship since his infancy. He, as well as Larry, frustrated easily and whenever he appeared unhappy Mrs. R. tended to blame herself for everything that went wrong. Her sense of worth was constantly being jeopardized by Mark's displeasure and complaints of not having anything to do. She usually interpreted his sad, troubled face as criticism and experienced rejection in response to his inability to express his feelings openly. She resented him for making demands on her that she felt she could not meet.

Mrs. R. looked upon her problems as a weakness and expressed extreme embarrassment about letting the therapist see her in a role other than that of a competent professional woman. Her discomfort was further increased by a bind she found herself in. She had the ever-present fear that if she didn't give into Mark's demands he would leave her to live with his own father. Consequently, she tended to give into him whenever she knew she shouldn't, and therefore seemed to reward him for his rejecting behavior. She discussed feelings of guilt about how she wished she could have done more for him when he was an infant. She was tortured by feelings of rejection and abandonment. When Mark was unable to talk about his feelings, she proceeded to question him in a way that he interpreted as intrusion, causing him to withdraw in anger and disgust. It appeared that each had a powerful message for the other in their non-verbal expressions. The mother's sad face of disappointment or disbelief and her son's tortured expression triggered an autonomic gut response in both; Mark felt "Now what have I done to let her down" and Mrs. R. felt inadequate and rejected.

As therapy proceeded, Mr. R. began to feel more comfortable with himself and was better able to express his feelings openly. He was beginning to let his son do more for himself. The first step was taken when Larry was given the opportunity to walk to school alone. This was followed by removal of his restricted diet made possible by the therapist's reassurance that Larry would not die as the result of an attack of diarrhea. After six months in therapy Mr. R. was beginning to have a better understanding of his own need to stay in control and finally allowed his son to suffer previously stated consequences if he failed to dress himself in time for school or for family outings. Helping Mr. R. with his discomfort in relinquishing control was a slow process. He was a very thrifty man who did all the shopping for the family. He bought clothes for himself and the children on sale. He said, "If I ever started spending money, I would not know when to stop." As a youngster he had worked hard and had been on his own since high school. He believed that "time is money" and therefore time should not be wasted by the children. They were not allowed to sleep late in the mornings even during the summer or on vacation. This thriftiness bothered Mrs. R. At the time the following conversation took place Mrs. R. complained about how her husband had bought his former wife a $300 coat.

Mrs. R.: I always watch what I buy. I'm careful. I pay for my own clothes. I'm very practical. (sanctimonious, resentful voice) However, I do feel that the children should get things without having to know the price and should receive things as gifts and not always have to pay for what they get. I don't ask for a $300 coat.

Therapist: What you're saying is that if your husband really loved you he would give you a $300 coat. That is, if you're really worth it. (As a release of tension, everyone laughed and she was able to laugh at herself.)

Mrs. R. was extremely jealous of the attention her husband gave others, never quite sure where she stood with him. The following conversation occurred after Mr. R. talked with Larry's mother on the phone about her poor relationship with Larry.

Mrs. R. (directed to her husband): I don't ever want you to speak to her again.

Therapist: That sounds like an ultimatum. You must be terribly threatened, jealous, and angry.

As stated earlier, Larry felt empty and abandoned by his own mother who lavished expensive presents every Christmas and gave him money on her rare visits. His problems of frustration and hyperactivity seemed to increase as he longed to see her. He had a fantasy that mother's love meant indulgence and money. His own mother never called him and never initiated the visit, always leaving the responsibility up to him.   Larry never felt successful in his attempts to initiate visits.   He hoped each phone call at home would be from his own mother.   Two months after Christmas he became unmanageable at home and he began to direct his withdrawn, angry, non-verbal behavior towards his female teacher at school.   Regular visits were arranged for Larry with his mother which calmed him down.

Meanwhile, Mark, his stepbrother, seemed happier and was better able to express his feelings openly.   Mark was allowed to visit his father more frequently and he was told that even though he may feel like he would like to run away and live with his father,   his   home was with his mother and stepfather.

Mrs. R. made unreasonable demands upon herself as though she were a superwoman.   She was a perfectionist and expected perfection in herself and others.   When others did not meet her expectations,   she became easily hurt and vindictive.   Her vindictiveness was shown by criticism and expressions of disappointment and disillusionment.   It was apparent that her children and husband were feeling the heavy burden and responsibility of protecting her from disappointment.

Although a positive change in the way Mrs. R. felt about herself had already begun, a noticeable change followed a particular role playing incident in therapy.   During this time Mark was made aware of his mother's inability to ask for anything for herself, and he learned that she had extremely low self-esteem and that his expressions of frustration made her feel inadequate.

As   stated   earlier,   role   playing   is   an

effective method to improve self-awareness and communication. This technique was used with Mrs. R. when she was feeling worthless, unable to ask for anything for herself because she felt non-deserving. The "Non-deserving Mrs. R." was asked to tell off the "Deserving Mrs. R." who was theoretically sitting in an empty chair. The role was reversed and Mrs. R. moved to the empty chair to play the opposite side of herself. This became a very touching moment. The "Deserving Mrs. R." had nothing to say, only the "Non-deserving Mrs. R." had a voice. An underlying theme of her life surfaced--the feeling of being worthless and non-deserving. This feeling was experienced in such a dramatic way that she could understand both emotionally and intellectually what an absurd position she found herself in. She began to understand her need to be perfect and how this perfection allowed for no mistakes in herself and others. From this point on, she began to appear more real and dropped her smiling facade in subsequent visits. Her dress and posture appeared more natural and she seemed to be in closer touch with her own feelings. She began making more reasonable demands of herself.

The family prospered in therapy, with each small change making each subsequent change possible. If nothing else, this family demonstrates the complex nature of children's learning and behavior problems and the need to work within the framework of the family system to understand and cope with the many factors at play. Fortunately, Larry made it possible for the family to avail themselves of help. Mrs. R.'s pride prevented her from seeking help for herself and her son and she had been thinking of divorce at the time they first came in. She had felt Larry's demands took time and love away from her own son.

There was a series of unexpected devel-

opments, one after another. Each parent's
unresolved intrapsychic conflicts or unfinished
business determined what they did at any one
moment and seriously affected their function
within the family. Both parents learned during
therapy that they needed each other in the
management of their own child. One could not
exclude the other. The children needed their
parents to lead from strength. Contrary to the
first impression, the father and son were not
the only ones with problems; each parent came
to the marriage with a disturbed parent-child
relationship. The parents learned through open
communication that they could help each other
and in this way help the relationship between
themselves. Towards the end of therapy a
gradual shift had occurred in the parents roles.
The father had learned to deal with his conflicts over control and allowed his wife to
mother his child. She, on the other hand,
was helped to resolve her conflicts of worth
which allowed her to ask Mr. R. to act as
father to her son.

The final stage of therapy was spent with
Mrs. R. in working through some of the terrible
experiences she had had as a child which
accounted for her feelings of worthlessness.
As she became more confident, she felt less
threatened by the imperfections in herself and
others and it became easier for her to "let go"
of Mark which actually brought him closer. As
she learned to take care of herself from a
position of strength, Mark no longer had to be
everything to his mother and she was able to
prevent him from taking advantage of her and
therefore he felt more comfortable.

This case and the others discussed in the text
demonstrate the therapeutic effectiveness of a comprehensive neurodevelopmental-family approach to the understanding and management of childhood learning and behavior
problems. From the use of a process-oriented, non-
categorical assessment, the vulnerable child and his

parents are protected from the blame and labeling that frequently occur in the existing adversary dilemma of professional either/or-ism.   If this approach is not used, the parents' search for help often ends with increased conflict rather than resolution.   The unique advantages of this approach not only places an emphasis on process rather than content, it considers together the child's inherent ability to learn and develop language function and the dynamic interaction of the family system as two important determinants of childhood behavior and experience. Therapy proceeds,   therefore,   from   the   non-categorical   process assessment of child development and family function.   It provides useful information about what is going on so that change can follow for more effective individual function and improved family interaction.

Appendix I

Expanded Neurological Examination for the School Age Child--An Operational Guide

1. Size and General Appearance - observe:
   General health and nutrition
   Physical characteristics
   Style of dress
   Hygiene
   Habit patterns
   Apparent age versus chronological age
   Projected gender role
   Mannerisms and gestures, autoerotic movements, tics

2. Activity Level - Observe state under various conditions
   Hyper- or hypokinesis
   Distractibility

3. Involuntary Movements
   Tremors - resting or intention (cerebellar) (shown by finger-nost test and handwriting)
   Choreoathetoid movements - at rest and in movement (cerebellar)

4. Coordination and Posture - Motor Strengths and Tone
   Gross motor coordination quality, i.e., graceful, clumsy
   Posture and gait
   Heel walk
   Tiptoe walk
   Tandem walk - forward and backward (age 6)
   Hopping - one foot, both feet
   Skipping (test of coordination and sequential planning)

89

Arm extension test (mature response depends on maturity of entire motor system) - test in sitting position, arms horizontal and parallel, eyes closed; normal response (after age 8) both arms deviate upward and laterally 1-5 cm/20 sec., dominant hand for writing deviates slightly more than non-dominant

Head rotation test or "neck righting response" (mature response depends on integrity of entire motor system) - test in standing position, eyes closed, feet together, arms extended, passively rotate head to one side as far as possible without discomfort; test both directions of rotation; normal response (after age 8) chin arm deviates upward slightly, both arms follow chin rotation

Rapid alternating movements
    Test for adiadochokinesis
    Doorknob rattle
    Lightbulb twist
Heel-shin test

Dysfunctional findings in tests of gross motor coordination: poor balance, posturing, clumsiness, asymmetry of associated arm swing or co-movements,
        Restriction: spasticity or rigidity (corticospinal or extra-pyramidal dysfunction)
        Flailing: associated with hypotonia and possible cerebellar dysfunction
        Athetoid: bizarre rotation of arm and/or flexion or extension of hand (extrapyramidal dysfunction

Fine motor coordination
    Finger-thumb test (speed, accuracy, sequence)
    Writing and drawing (pencil grip)

5. Abnormal Associated Movements (mirror movements,
      synkinesia)
         Observe opposite side of body during finger-
            thumb and rapid alternating movements
            tests for fragmentary movements which
            mirror those of the test side; may be
            minimally present up through age 10; sig-
            nificant when grossly exaggerated beyond
            6 years

6. Higher Cerebral Functions
         Two-point discrimination (dual simultaneous
            sensory tests or "face-hand" tests of
            Bender) - touch simultaneously, eyes
            closed, child points to the spots touched,
            e.g., (a) both cheeks, (b) both hands,
            (c) cheek and homolateral hand, (d) cheek
            and contralateral hand, (e) opposites of c
            and d; dysfunctional responses (after age
            5-6) parietal lobe dysfunction: rostral
            dominance (failure to perceive hand
            stimulus when face is simultaneously
            touched), extinction (failure to perceive
            one stimulus when opposite parts of body
            are simultaneously touched), displacement
            (grossly defective localization of one
            stimulus)
         Self-awareness of body in space - directional
            sense, position sense, body image
            Right-left discrimination - ability to
               identify right and left at age 5 or 6
               and that of the examiner; when dys-
               functional, child is considered to
               have confused laterality
            Dominance - hand used for writing, eating;
               foot used in kicking
            Finger localization test - touch two fingers
               or two spots on one finger simul-
               taneously, eyes closed; child points
               to spots touched (parietal lobe func-
               tion); normal when 5 or more correct
               out of 8 trials on each side
            Imitation of gestures (age 6) - reflects
               finger discrimination, postural praxis,

awareness of self-image, spatial organization of movement: personal-extrapersonal, right-left, front-back, up-down orientation (parietal lobe function); mirror movements can be present up to age 8

One-hand tests: (a) extend little finger or thumb, (b) extend little finger and index finger, (c) extend index finger and middle finger, (d) fist-edge-palm test, (e) fingertips to chin

Two-hand tests: (a) fist-palm, (b) fingertips-palm, (c) finger in hole

Graphasia - write numbers or letters 2-3 cm. size on thenar eminence, eyes closed; must recognize 3 out of 4 on each hand

7. Reflexes
       Look for asymmetry of deep tendon reflexes

8. Toe signs

9. Cranial nerves - check for:
       Visual acuity
       Strabismus
       Nystagmus
       Facial weakness
       Dysarthria
       Swallow
       Whistle
       Close one eye

10. Balance - modification of Romberg Test: items derived from Lincoln-Oseretsky Motor Development Scale (tests for static postural control)
       Stand on one foot for 10 seconds with eyes closed (age 6) (cerebellar function)

11. Speech
       Watch for obvious receptive or expressive language disorders, auditory acuity and discrimination, articulation deficits, dis-

orders of intonation, grammar, speech
pattern, pitch, dysfluency, pronomial
reversal and gender confusion

*

Bibliography

Bender, M. B. Disorders in perception. Springfield, Ill.:
　　Thomas, 1952.
Benton, A. L. Right-left discrimination and finger local-
　　ization. New York: Hoeber, 1959.
Berges, J. and Lezine, I. The imitation of gestures.
　　London: Heinemann, 1965.
Gamstorp, I. Pediatric neurology. New York: Appleton-
　　Century-Crofts, 1970.
Goodman, J. D. and Sours, J. A. The child mental status
　　examination. New York: Basic Books, 1967.
Kinsbourne, M. and Warrington, E. K. A study of finger
　　agnosia. Brain, 1962, 85, 47-66.
Sloan, W. The Lincoln-Oseretsky motor development
　　scale. Genet. Psychol. Monographs, 1955, 51,
　　183-252.
Steegman, A. T. Examination of the nervous system.
　　(2nd ed.) Chicago: Year Book Medical Publishers,
　　1962.

Appendix II

Tests Used in the Developmental Assessment

OBSERVED BEHAVIOR:
    Attention
    Attitude
    Distractibility
    Motor Activity
    Performance Quality
    Performance Speed
    Problem-solving Methods
    Rapport
    Response Control
    Response to Failure
    Task Needs
    Verbal Activity

EDUCATIONAL ACHIEVEMENT:
    Wide Range Achievement Test (WRAT)
        Reading Grade (isolated word recognition)
        Spelling Grade (writing dictated words)
        Arithmetic Grade (written computation)
        Authors: J. Jastak, S. Bijou and S. Jastak
        Address of Publisher: Guidance Associates
                                     Wilmington, Delaware

GENERAL INTELLIGENCE:
    Wechsler Intelligence Scale for Children (WISC)
        Performance Scale I.Q.
        Verbal Scale I.Q.
        Full Scale I.Q.
        Author: David Wechsler
        Address of Publisher: The Psychological Corp.
                                     New York, New York

Stanford-Binet Intelligence Scale, Form L-M
 Author: L. W. Terman and M. A. Merrill
 Address of Publisher: Houghton Mifflin Co.
                                    Boston, Massachusetts

VISUAL-MOTOR FUNCTION:
 Bender Visual-Motor Gestalt Test
  Author: Lauretta Bender
  Address of Publisher: American Orthopsychiatric
                                     Association, Inc.
                                     New York, New York

 Developmental Test of Visual-Motor Integration
  Author: Keith E. Beery
  Address of Publisher: Follett Educational Corp.
                                     Chicago, Illinois

 Draw-A-Person (DAP)
  Author: William H. Urban
  Address of Publisher: Western Psychological
                                     Services
                                     Los Angeles, California

 Frostig Developmental Test of Visual Perception
  Author: M. Frostig
  Address of Publisher: Consulting Psychologists
                                     Press
                                     Palo Alto, California

VISUAL MEMORY:
 Detroit Test of Learning Aptitude
  Authors: H. J. Baker and B. Leland
  Address of Publisher: Bobbs-Merrill Co.
                                     Indianapolis, Indiana

 Benton Revised Visual Retention Test
  Author: Arthur Benton
  Address of Publisher: The Psychological Corp.
                                     New York, New York

 Illinois Test of Psycholinguistic Abilities (ITPA)
  Subtest: Visual Sequential Memory
  Authors: S. Kirk, J. McCarthy and W. Kirk
  Address of Publisher: Univ. of Illinois Press
                                     Urbana, Illinois

AUDITORY MEMORY:
    Spencer Sentence Memory
        Author: E. M. Spencer (This test was reported
                  by the author in her Ph.D. thesis com-
                  pleted at Northwestern University in
                  1958.)

    Detroit Test of Learning Aptitude
        Authors: H. J. Baker and B. Leland
        Address of Publisher: Bobbs-Merrill Co.
                               Indianapolis, Indiana

    Illinois Test of Psycholinguistic Abilities (ITPA)
        Subtest: Auditory Sequential Memory
        Authors: S. Kirk, J. McCarthy and W. Kirk
        Address of Publisher: Univ. of Illinois Press
                               Urbana, Illinois

    Wepman Auditory Discrimination Test
        Author: J. Wepman
        Address of Publisher: Language Research
                               Associates
                               Chicago, Illinois

LANGUAGE FUNCTION (receptive vocabulary):
    Peabody Picture Vocabulary Test (PPVT)
        Author: Lloyd M. Dunn
        Address of Publisher: Western Psychological
                               Services
                               Los Angeles, California

    Quick Scoring Test of Learning Capacity
        Address of Publisher: Department of Educational
                               Research
                               Ontario College of
                               Education
                               University of Toronto
                               Guidance Centre
                               Toronto, Ontario, Canada

EMOTIONAL STATUS:
    Thematic Apperception Test (TAT)
            Author: M. I. Stein
            Address of Publisher: Western Psychological
                                    Services
                                    Los Angeles, California

    Children's Apperception Test (CAT)
            Authors: L. Bellak and S. Sorel Bellak
            Address of Publisher: Western Psychological
                                    Services
                                    Los Angeles, California

    "If" Sentence Completion Test

Appendix III

Tests Used in the Educational Evaluation

Durrell Analysis of Reading Difficulty
    Author: D. Durrell
    Address of Publisher: Harcourt Brace Javanovich, Inc.
               New York, New York

Monroe Reading Achievement Test
    Author: Marion Monroe
    Address of Publisher: Houghton Mifflin Co.
               777 California Avenue
               Palo Alto, California

Gates-McKillop Reading Diagnostic Tests
    Authors: A. Gates and A. McKillop
    Address of Publisher: Bureau of Publications
               Columbia University Teachers
               College
               New York, New York

Grays Oral Reading Test
    Authors: W. S. Gray and H. M. Robinson
    Address of Publisher: Bobbs-Merrill Co., Inc.
               4300 W. 62nd Street
               Indianapolis, Indiana

Gilmore Oral Reading Test
    Author: John V. Gilmore
    Address of Publisher: Harcourt Brace Jovanovich, Inc.
               New York, New York

Wide Range Achievement Test (WRAT)
    Authors: J. Jastak, S. Bijou and S. Jastak
    Address of Publisher: Harcourt Brace Jovanovich, Inc.
               New York, New York

Reading Suggestions

Ackerman, N. W. Treating the Troubled Family. New York: Basic Books, Inc., 1966.

Allmond, B. W. & Gofman, H. F. Learning and language disorders in children, Part I: The preschool child and Part II: The school-age child. Current Problems in Pediatrics, 1971, Vol. 1, Nos. 10 & 11.

Bell, N. W. & Vogel, E. F. A Modern Introduction to the Family. New York: The Free Press, 1968.

Jackson, D. D. & Lederer, W. J. Mirages of Marriage. New York: W. W. Norton & Co., 1968.

Miller, E. Foundations of Child Psychiatry. New York: Pergamon Press, 1968.

Perls, F. S. Gestalt Therapy Verbatim. Lafayette, California: Real People Press, 1969.

Satir, V. Conjoint Family Therapy. Palo Alto, California: Science and Behavior Books, Inc., 1964.

Spiegel, J. Transactions--The Interplay Between Individual, Family, and Society. New York: Science House, 1971.

Stevenson, H. W., Hess, E. H., & Rheingold, H. L. Early Behavior--Comparative and Developmental Approaches. New York: John Wiley & Sons, Inc., 1967.

Acknowledgments

I am indebted to the following members of the Child Study Unit team who have contributed their knowledge and skill to my clinical experience:

Dr. Bayard W. Allmond, Jr., Assistant Director, Child Study Unit; Assistant Professor of Pediatrics

Mrs. Valerie Anthony, Educational Consultant, Reading and Language Development Clinic

Mrs. Wilma Buckman, Family Therapist, Child Study Unit; Associate Clinical Professor of Psychiatric Social Work in Pediatrics

Mrs. Mary Rita Crittenden, Psychologist, Child Study Unit

Dr. Richard Flower, Speech, Language and Hearing Consultant; Professor of Speech Pathology and Audiology, Department of Otolaryngology

Dr. Helen Gofman, Director, Child Study Unit; Associate Professor of Pediatrics

Mrs. Donya Harvin, Psychologist, Child Study Unit

Miss Diana Kennedy, Psychologist, Child Study Unit

Dr. Alan Leveton, Psychiatrist, Child Study Unit; Associate Clinical Professor of Pediatrics

Mrs. Susan Kellerman, Educational Consultant, Reading and Language Development Clinic

Mrs. Eleanore Sterne, Educational Consultant, Reading and Language Development Clinic

Mrs. Alice Jane Whitsell, Educational Consultant; Director of the Reading and Language Development Clinic

Dr. Leon Whitsell, Neurologist, Child Study Unit; Associate Clinical Professor of Pediatrics and Neurology

References

Ackerman, N. W. Social role and total personality. *American Journal of Orthopsychiatry*, 1951, 21, 1-17. (a)

Ackerman, N. W. *Treating the Troubled Family*. New York: Basic Books, Inc., 1966. (b)

Allmond, B. W. & Gofman, H. F. Learning and language disorders in children--Part I: The preschool child. *Current Problems in Pediatrics*, 1971, Vol. 1, No. 10.

Allmond, B. W. & Gofman, H. F. Learning and language disorders in children--Part II: The school-age child. *Current Problems in Pediatrics*, 1971, Vol. 1, No. 11.

Anastasi, A. Heredity, environment, and the question "how?". *Psychology Review*, 1958, 65, 197-208.

Bateman, B. Analysis of reading disability. Curriculum Bulletin, University of Oregon School of Education, 1967, Vol. 3, No. 278.

Bell, J. E. Family group therapist: An agent of change. *International Journal of Group Psychotherapy*, 1964, 14, 72-78.

Bell, N. W. & Vogel, E. F. The emotionally disturbed child as the family scapegoat. In N. W. Bell & E. F. Vogel (Ed.) *A Modern Introduction to the Family*. New York: The Free Press, 1968, 412-427. (a)

Bell, N. W. & Vogel, E. F. Toward a framework for functional analysis of family behavior. In N. W. Bell & E. F. Vogel (Ed.) *A Modern Introduction to the Family*. New York: The Free Press, 1968, 1-34. (b)

Bender, L. Specific reading disability as a maturational lag. Bulletin of the Orton Society, 1957, 7, 9-18.

Berberich, J., Lovaas, I., Peiloff, B., & Schaffer, B. Acquisition of imitative speech by schizophrenic children. Science, 1966, 151, 705-707.

Carmichael, L. The onset of early development of behavior. In L. Carmichael (Ed.) Manual of Child Psychology. New York: John Wiley and Sons, Inc., 1954.

Clements, R. L. Syndromes of minimal brain dysfunction in children. Maryland Medical Journal, 1966, 15, 139-140.

Clements, S. D. & Peters, J. E. Minimal brain dysfunction in the school-age child. Archives of General Psychiatry, 1962, 6, 185-197.

DeHirsch, K., Jansky, J., & Langford, W. Predicting Reading Failure in the Pre-school Child. New York: Harper & Row, 1966.

Eibl-Eibesfeldt, I. Concepts of ethology and their significance in the study of human behavior. In H. W. Stevenson, E. H. Hess, & H. L. Rheingold (Ed.) Early Behavior--Comparative and Developmental Approaches. New York: John Wiley & Sons, Inc., 1967, 127-146.

Eisenberg, L. Basic issues in drug research with children; Opportunities and limitations of a pediatric age group. In S. Fisher (Ed.) Child research in psychopharmacology, Springfield, Ill.: Charles C. Thomas, 1959, 21-42.

Eisenberg, L. Psychopharmacology in childhood: A critique. In E. Miller (Ed.) Foundations of Child Psychiatry, Oxford, Edinberg, Long Island: Pergamon Press, 1968, 625-641.

Erikson, E. H. Childhood and Society. New York: W. W. Norton & Co., 1950, 44-92 & 219-234.

Escalona, S. K. The study of individual differences and the problem of state. Journal of the American Academy of Child Psychiatry, 1962, 1, 11-37.

Ferreira, A. J. Family myth and homeostasis. Archives of General Psychiatry, 1963, 9, 457-463.

Fowler, G. W. & Millichap, J. G. Treatment of "minimal brain dysfunction" syndromes: Selection of drugs for children with hyperactivity and learning disabilities. Pediatric Clinics of North America, 1967, 4, 767-777.

Freedman, D. G. Smiling in blind infants and the issues of innate vs acquired. _Journal Child Psychol. Psychiatr._, 1964, 5, 171-184.

Freedman, D. G. Hereditary control of early social behavior. In B. M. Foss (Ed.) _Determinants of Infant Behavior._ London: Methuen, 1965.

Freud, A. Indications for child analysis. _The Psychoanalytic Study of the Child_, 1945, 1, 127-149.

Gehrke, S. & Kirschenbaum, M. Survival patterns in family conjoint therapy. _Family Process_, 1967, 6, 67-80.

Gesell, The ontogenesis of infant behavior.   In L. Carmichael (Ed.) _Manuel of Child Psychology_. New York: John Wiley and Sons, Inc., 1954, 335-373.

Gomez, M. R. Minimal cerebral dysfunction (maximal neurological confusion). _Clinical Pediatrics_, 1967, 6, 589-591.

Goodenough, F. L. Expressions of the emotions in a blind-deaf child. _Journal of Abnormal Social Psychology_, 1932, 27, 328-333.

Greenberg, L. W. The hyperactive child. _California Medicine_, 1971, 115, 43. (Abstract)

Griffin, M. E., Johnson, A. M., & Litin, E. M. The transmission of superego defects in the family. _American Journal of Orthopsychiatry_, 1954, 24, 668-684. Cited in Bell, N. W. & Vogel, E. F. (Ed.) _A Modern Introduction to the Family._ New York: The Free Press, 1968, 670-682.

Haley, J. Experiment with abnormal families. _Archives of General Psychiatry_, 1967, 17, 53-63.

Haley, J. The longitudinal family cycle. Paper presented at the Seventh Annual Symposium of the California State Marriage Counseling Association, San Francisco, October 1970.

Institute for Development of Educational Activities, Inc. The role of the ophthalmologist in dyslexia. Dayton, Ohio: Institute for Development of Educational Activities, Inc., 1969, p 7.

Jackson, D. D. The question of family homeostasis. _Psychiatric Quarterly_, 1957, 79-90. (Suppl. 1957)

Jespersen, O. Die Sprache, Heidelburg, 1925.

Johnson, A. M. & Szurek, S. A. The genesis of acting out in children and adults. _Psychoanalytic Quarterly_, 1952, 21, 323-343.

Kanner, L.   Autistic disturbances of affective contact. Nerv. Child., 1943, 2, 217-250.

Katz, D.   Animals and Men--Studies in Comparative Psychology. New York: Longman, Green & Co., 1937.

Kaufman, I., Peck, A. L., & Tagiuri, C. K.   The family constellations and overt incestuous relations between father and daughter. American Journal of Orthopsychiatry, 1954, 24, 266-277. Cited by N. W. Bell & E. F. Vogel (Ed.) in A Modern Introduction to the Family. New York: The Free Press, 1968, 569-609. (a)

Kaufman, I., Peck, A. L., & Tagiuri, C. K.   Implicit stimulation and implicit permission. American Journal of Orthopsychiatry, 1954, 24, 226-227. (b)

Kessen, W.   Patterns of behavior in the human newborn. In H. W. Stevenson, E. H. Hess, & H. L. Rheingold (Ed.) Early Behavior--Comparative and Developmental Approaches. New York: John Wiley and Sons, Inc., 1967, 147-149.

Koehler.   Das Lachelm al angeborene Ausdrucksbewegung - X. meusch. Verebu - Konst. Lehre., 1954, 32, 330-334.

Laing, R. D.   The Politics of Experience. New York: Ballantine Books, Inc., 1967.

LaVeck, G.   Learning disorders in children. Report of the Sixty-First Ross Conference on Pediatric Research, Columbus, Ohio: Ross Laboratories, 1970, 25-26.

Lipsitt, L. P.   Learning in the human infant. In H. W. Stevenson, E. H. Hess, & H. L. Rheingold Early Behavior--Comparative and Developmental Appoaches. New York: John Wiley & Sons, Inc., 1967, 225-247.

Malmquist, C. P.   Depressions in childhood and adolescence. New England Journal of Medicine, 1971, Vol. 284, Nos. 16 & 17, 887-893 & 955-961.

McBride, G.   The nature-nurture problem in social evolution. Paper presented at the Smithsonian Institution Third International Symposium entitled Man and Beast: Comparative Social Behavior, Washington, D. C., 1969.

Millichap, G. J.   Drugs in the management of hyperkinetic and perceptually handicapped children. Journal of the American Medical Association, 1968, 7, 1527-1530.

Morgan, W. P.   A case of congenital word blindness. British Medical Journal, 1896, 2, 1378.

Orton, S. T.   Reading, Writing, and Speech Problems in Children. New York: W. W. Norton & Co., 1937.

Peiper, A.   Cerebral function in infancy and childhood. New York: Consultants Bureau, 1961.   (Translated in 1963 from Schreit-und Steigbewegungen beim Neugelborenen. Archives Kinderh, 1953, 147, p 135.)

Perls, F. S., Hefferline, R. F., & Goodman, P.   Gestalt Therapy. New York: Dell Publishing Co., Inc., 1951.

Perls, F. S.   Gestalt Therapy Verbatim.   Lafayette, California: Real People Press, 1969.

Piaget, J.   The Origins of Intelligence in Children. New York: International University Press, 1936.

Prechtl, H. F. R. & Schleidt, W.   Auslosende und steuernde mechanismen des saugaktes. Z. Vgl. Physiol., 1950, 33, 53-62.

Rimland, B.   Infantile Autism. New York: Appleton - Century - Crofts, Inc., 1964, 94-96.

Sander, L. W.   Issues in early mother-child interaction. Journal of the American Academy of Child Psychiatry, 1962, 1, 141-166.

Satir, V.   Conjoint Family Therapy. Palo Alto, California: Science and Behavior Books, Inc., 1964.

Scheerenberger, R. C.   Mental retardation: Definition, classification, and prevalence.   Mental Retardation Abstracts, 1964, 1, 1-10.

Schilder, P.   Contributions to Developmental Neuro-psychiatry. New York: International University Press, 1960.

Spitz, R. A.   The smiling response: A contribution to the ontogenesis of social relations. Genetic Psychology Monograph, 1946, 34, 57-125.

Stoller, R. J.   Sex and Gender--On the Development of Masculinity and Femininity. New York: Science House, 1969.

Szurek, S. A.   Notes on the genesis of psychopathic personality trends. Psychiatry, 1942, 5, 1-6.

Taichert, L. C.   Specific learning disorders--natural history and current views. California Medicine, 1968, 109, 286-290.

Taichert, L. C.   Childhood   encopresis--a   neurodevelop-
    mental-family approach to management.   California
    Medicine, 1971, 115, 11-18.
Whitsell, L. J.   Learning disorders as a school health
    problem.   California Medicine, 1969, 111, 433-445.
Wolff, P. H.   The role of biological rhythms in early
    psychological development.   Bulletin of the Menninger
    Clinic, 1967, 31, 197-218.

Index

370.15
T 129

112 894